LEADERSHIP IS

By

Harrison Owen

ABBOTT PUBLISHING

Potomac, Maryland

First published 1990

ABBOTT PUBLISHING
7808 River Falls Drive
Potomac, MD 20854
301-469-9269

Printed in the United States of America

Library of Congress Catalog Card Number 90-080143
ISBN 0-9618205-1-9

TABLE OF CONTENTS

Preface

This book is about leadership and spirit, or maybe spirited leadership. Although its sources are many, and too numerous to acknowledge, the book is finally the product of my own reflections on the subject, based upon a prime conviction that *Spirit* is the essential reality. Thus, while I begin with several considerations of eminent practicality, in addition to the "no news" observation concerning the present lack of leadership, I end in places that some may find strange. I say all this, not by way of apology, but rather under the heading of *caveat emptor.* I take leadership and spirit with the utmost seriousness, and I do not think that the former can be dealt with apart from the latter.

You will not find here a new version of "Seven Magic Steps to Powerful Leadership." I invite you, however, to join me on a journey that I have found to be both exciting and rewarding. I am clear that the final word on leadership has yet to be spoken, and certainly this book will not change that reality.

This is a story, and as such, attempts less to tell the truth (facts) about leadership, than to create a space in which the truth may be encountered. All of which means that if you do not like my story, please tell your own. I would hope, however that my tale might enrich the telling of yours. One good story always deserves another.

Harrison Owen
Potomac, Maryland
1989

CHAPTER I

WHERE HAVE ALL THE LEADERS GONE?

"Where have all the leaders gone?" That could well be the song for the last part of the 20th century. In the national press scarcely a day passes without extended discussion of the lack of leadership and the apparent inability of the major political parties to raise up anyone who remotely looks the part.

Corporate America is in little better shape. With the possible exception of Lee Iacocca, the strong, charismatic, decisive Leader of yesteryear has seemingly been replaced by gray men. Bold strokes have given way to defensive strategies, aimed less at defining the future than preserving the past.

Indeed, to the extent that heroes and leaders of the people still populate the planet, at least the American portion of the planet, they appear to be, likely as not, rogues: the corporate raiders and other folks who live by the Darwinian law of survival. Brandishing their leveraged buy-outs, they add another notch in their guns.

As we sing our song and look for leaders, we find vast numbers of willing guides and commentators. Books and courses on leaders and leadership seem to have risen in inverse proportion to our perception of available talent. We are counseled how to take charge, be assertive, don the charismatic cloak, and other sure-fire methods for slaying dragons and summoning popular support. But for all the courses and training time, it seems that the refrain is still to be sung, "Where have all the leaders gone?"

The current "crisis in leadership" is genuine, but its cause may be more a matter of our perception. There is no question that leaders, as we have we have always known them, are in short supply. But we might ask if something has gone wrong with the genetic pool, such that *Homo sapiens* no longer possesses the capacity to lead. Or could it be that the times have changed, and leadership, "as it used to be," is no longer appropriate?

Here is my story. As the structures of our world, and the conditions of certainty, yield to an avalanche of change, the extent of our longing for stable, definitive leadership is exceeded only by the impossibility of finding it. The fault lies not with our leaders, but rather with ourselves, and our expectations. In the old days, leaders were supposed to make sense of chaos, certainty of doubt, and were to create positive action plans for the resolution of imponderable paradoxes. Good leaders straightened things out. Should chaos rear its ugly head, the leader was expected to restore normality immediately.

But there's the rub. Chaos is now "normal," paradoxes cannot be resolved, and certainty is possible only to the level of high probability. Leadership that attempts to deliver in terms of fixing any of this can only fail. And that is exactly what is happening.

HAVE THE LEADERS REALLY GONE?

Now, suppose we were to twist things around a bit, even at the risk of charges of "polyannaism." As strange as our world appears at the moment, and despite all the obvious risks now present, isn't it quite remarkable that we appear to be muddling through as well as we are? To the extent that leadership is necessary to survival, perhaps leadership is not as absent as we thought.

The list of impending disasters, potential and actual, is long: nuclear holocaust, acid rain, holes in the ozone, overpopulation, famine, chemical wastes, the greenhouse effect, omnipresent carcinogens, decertification, and a variety of other planetary catastrophes. On a more human level we confront such difficulties as financial collapse, monumental national debt, plant closings, downsizing, restructures, takeovers, and the elimination of entire industries. Were one given to pessimism, there is enough material here to legitimize a massive state of depression. Yet, for all that is going wrong, will go wrong, or could go wrong, the fact remains that we seem to be making it, one way or another. Rather like Mark Twain, we may remark that the report of our imminent demise is premature. And to the extent that leadership is now, as always, necessary for our survival, one might suspect that it is still present — somehow.

Obviously *Homo sapiens*, and indeed the small Planet Earth, could cease to exist tomorrow morning, or sooner. But that has always been true, if not for reasons of our own stupidity, then because of some aberrant asteroid. Yet for several billion years, Planet Earth and its passengers have survived, one might say prospered. Contrary to every prediction of immediate disaster to date, we are still here. What on earth, we may ask, is going on? What would we be doing, if we thought what we were doing made sense?

What would we be doing, if we thought what we were doing made sense?

WHAT ON EARTH IS GOING ON?

We are doing what we've always done; we are transforming. In one way or another, with or without our own permission, we are headed down the path we have always been meant to follow, toward the fulfillment of our human potential.

There is, of course, no guarantee that we are finally going to make it.

The process of transformation is not always pleasant, indeed it can be downright terrifying. For transformation means that the old forms of our existence are blown apart, and put aside, creating *open space* within which a new expression of us may emerge. For those who have found their meaning exclusively in the forms and structures of life, the experience is actually beyond terror, for it appears that life itself is about to cease. And in truth, life as *it was*, comes to an end. That is chaos, but it also may be the nutrient seed bed from which new life will emerge.

And what of leadership? Two versions of the leadership tale are told currently. The first is one we have been telling for some time, in which the few, or even The One, have all the answers, and therefore the power, to protect us from chaos. In his or her strength, we learn, and/or are forced to do, *the right thing*, which will assure the preservation of life as we have come to expect it. Order and stability are the fruits of our obedience, and a full belly, a full garage, and lifetime employment are the anticipated rewards. And when, at a time such as now, order and stability are mostly apparent in their absence, we look about for some suitable object of blame. That blame object is not far away. There is a lack of leadership, for if that were not true, so goes the story, things would obviously be better than they are. Perhaps.

But there is another story in which leadership is not the exclusive property of the few or the One. Questions, not answers predominate, and the right thing is no *thing* at all. In this story, there is no lack of leadership, but rather the emergent presence of a very different sort of leadership. It is new, really there, and really effective. Leadership under the conditions of transformation is a collective, and constantly re-distributed function, and not the private property of the few or The One. The role of leadership is to engage in the quest (pose the *question*) for the realization of human potential. And the goal of leadership is not the establishment of some perfect state (the Right Thing), but rather the heightened quality of the journey itself. The secret is out. We are all leaders, and there are plenty of us. At least, that is this story.

CHAPTER II

TRANSFORMATION:
THE CONTEXT OF LEADERSHIP

Transformation is occurring now. Not later, not soon, but right this instant. Of course it has always been so, for the history of the species has been an ongoing journey of the evolution of consciousness: the transformation of our essence from one form to a new one. From the moment we branched from our brothers and sisters in the remainder of the Animal Kingdom, indeed from the moment before that moment, when animal and plant became distinct entities, transformation has been occurring. Truth to tell, it all began, if it began at all, in that fiery instant of pure energy expanding infinitely across nothingness. And who knows, maybe it never began, but always was. But whatever the point of genesis, Transformation is not new.

What is new, or at least what strikes us as strange, is the *rate* of transformation. There clearly have been times when things seemed never to change. Perhaps appearances were deceiving, or we were deceived by our own lack of awareness, but it certainly seemed that yesterday, today and tomorrow were all of a piece. Our deception was probably self-induced. No one, and no thing, likes to change, for all systems are essentially conservative. So it may well be that we have played the ancient and honorable game of the emperor's clothes.

Everybody knew the emperor was naked, but none dared say so.

However things have been, they are surely different now. And the excitement and terror of the moment lie less in the actual difference, than in the speed with which the differences become manifest. We are riding the tiger to somewhere, and we no longer need the Tofflers and Naisbitts of this world to tell us so.[1] Our common, everyday experience is of a world in transformation, but if we need any further evidence, 1992 could be pivotal.

1992 AND ALL THAT

The year 1992, with the creation of the new European Market, means radical alteration in business as it used to be. In one instant, trade barriers fall, and a new marketplace, with 325 million folks, is inaugurated. The final nature and impact of this change remains to be made clear, but at this juncture it is apparent that every trading relationship and business practice is up for reconsideration. Not that they all will pass away, but for sure the context will be different. That means the issues and opportunities will come in different packages.

For businesses in Europe, the old Balkanized relationships, outmoded as they may have been, were nevertheless known and for that reason, comfortable. They will

---

[1] John Naisbitt, <u>Megatrends - Ten New Directions Transforming Our Lives</u> (Warner Books, 1982). Alvin Toffler, <u>Future Shock</u> (Bantam Books, 1970).

be replaced. What comes next has never been known, and in a very real sense cannot be dealt with in advance. January 1, 1992 creates a whole new economic reality.

Even as Europe moves toward that magical moment when everything in principle changes, the United States and Canada have embarked on a similar path. Further to the east, the Pacific Rim nations, headed by Japan Inc. and closely followed by Korea and Taiwan, continue in a dynamic path of growth and development. To a remarkable extent, they already dominate the world economy, if not in total value traded, then at least in perception. Scarcely a day goes by, in either North America or Europe, when the Japanese and their colleagues are not held up as the best available *bête noire*, on which to blame virtually anything that does not seem to be going well in the local economic picture.

Completing the tour around the globe requires acknowledging the emerging sounds of a new spirit coming from the Eastern Block countries. Under the code names of *perestroika* and *glasnost*, something quite different has come into being. Some may see this as the final gasp of a dying system which has effectively strangled itself in a tangle of bureaucratic constraints, but "last gasp" or "fresh breath" it is clear that the winds of change are blowing.

Of course there is one more piece in the emerging global stew: China. China stands alone. The self-imposed isolation of the past 30 years is coming to an end, and a major question arises: What will happen when one billion Chinese join the global market? Despite their presently underdeveloped state, and the bloodshed in Beijing, it remains true that the resources, (physical, intellectual and spiritual) of that people are truly staggering. The mind boggles at the potential impact of a full and intentional Chinese entry onto the global stage.

As the various parts of the world move toward their own new working relationships, we will experience a period of local consolidation, as each becomes accustomed to the new order. But the net impact of the new working relationships will be seen less in terms of their local impact than *the total synergistic effect*. We are, after all, residents of the same planet. Thus, if the impact of 1992 appears awesome for the European participants, the effect will be no less awesome for all other members of the global community — as common Europe interacts with common North America, and both in turn with the Pacific Rim, and the nations of the Eastern Block. Throw in the giant question mark of the People's Republic of China, and the stew becomes profoundly rich and unknowable.

NEW RULES

There is much in our common global history which suggests that the new interrelationships will be but a logical extrapolation from what we have always known. Instead of having 150-plus nation-states defending their boundaries and, simultaneously, attempting to breach the boundaries of others, thereby to gain a trading advantage, we now will have only four or five entities all engaged in the same.

I believe this scenario to be flawed. Despite the potential comfort gained in knowing that the basic rules remain inviolate, many confounding factors render the hope futile. I mention only two: the multinational (global) corporations and the Electronic Revolution.

Global Business

The multinational corporations have already removed the nation-state from its previous role as the *only* player in the global economic environment. The several nation-states have significant roles to play, but no longer do the states "context" the corporations; rather the reverse occurs. Put more clearly, it used to be the case that a particular business was German, French or American, and did business in the global community as a "representative" of that country. In many ways, this situation was merely a holdover from colonial days when, for example, the English crown was represented in the New World, not only by the resident colonial governor (high commissioner), but also by the Hudson Bay Trading Company, which held its charter from the Crown. In that case, the country provided the context (identity) for the corporation.

Things have now changed. For a large multinational, operating simultaneously in many countries, it may still be superficially true that it is an "American company," but at a deeper level it is a global institution with its own identity, quite independent of the nation of origin, or the nations in which it happens to be doing business. The center of identity lies no longer with the *country* but with the *company*, which now provides the context of operations.

Obviously, there is a spectrum of effect, with some companies still maintaining strong national ties. Rolls Royce is unmistakably British. Other corporations, however, are no longer even multinational, they are in effect global. Electrolux is thought by many Americans to be an American company, although in fact it has its roots in Sweden. Major oil companies, typically, are far along the road to global identity. Shell Oil, was from the beginning a British Dutch effort, although its many national manifestations appear quite indigenous. For the American consumer, Shell is just one more gas station. From Shell's point of view, it is a global network having a broad range of national embodiments. The difference may only be perception, but in the case of the emerging global economic community, how we think about such issues will be determinative.

The Electronic Revolution

The electronic revolution adds another dimension to the emerging global environment. Since the advent of workable computers at the close of World War II, we have all had the sneaking suspicion that things would never be the same again. The doomsayers predicted a world monitored by big brother, and the optimists foresaw instant communication and harmony. Neither turned out to be right, but the world certainly is different. For a long time that difference was quietly hidden in the back-room data processing centers, where little men in white coats guarded the sanctuary. Now it seems the computers have escaped their keepers, and we all know by experience what we have long suspected. The world isn't what it used to be.

Should any doubt remain, the events of October 19, 1987 stand as a watershed. On one level, we witnessed a global

12

financial disaster of previously unimaginable proportions. The American market lost 25 percent of its value, and other markets registered declines of twice that amount. In the United States alone, one half a trillion dollars simply disappeared in 24 hours, representing just about half of the total United States federal budget.

Curiously, when all the smoke had cleared, very little seemed to have happened. Except for stockbrokers and investors playing out on the margins, almost everything else came through in good shape. Should we then call October 19 a non-event? In financial terms possibly, but as a global learning experience it was a megabuster.

In 24 hours, anybody who had access to the public media witnessed the electronic revolution firsthand. As our small globe turned before the sun, one marketplace after another signed on to the great computer conference in the sky, did its business, and retired from the field of battle. But the electronic marketplace never stopped. New York, London, Tokyo, each made an appearance and disappeared, but the real market rolled on.

For those invested in the certainty of time and a place, the events of the day were shattering, for suddenly it became apparent that the comings and goings on Wall Street, for example, were but part of the show, which had meaning only as a piece of the larger electronic fabric. Indeed if one were to boldly ask, "Where and when was the market?" the inescapable answer was, *The market was whenever, and wherever, anybody wanted it.* You certainly didn't have to be in London, Tokyo, or New York. Given a phone line and a Personal Computer, access was provided. So where *really* is the market? Obviously, in the Great Electronic Connection.

A shocking day, all in all, for the financial markets of the world.[2] Not only did they take a beating monetarily, even worse, they discovered their own irrelevance. But for the rest of us, the news and the learnings can be useful. Unless the planet suffers a huge, and permanent, electrical short-circuit, otherwise known as nuclear disaster, we may presume that the electronic revolution will continue, broaden and intensify. This means that all of us, not just the select few, will be party to a different reality, the electronic connection, in which time and space no longer mean what they used to. One might ask: Is this real? To which the only reasonable answer appears to be: Well, it was certainly real enough to vanish a half a trillion dollars (to say nothing of additional yen, marks and francs) on a single day.

The implications for our emerging Super Markets, and all those who choose to do business therein, are profound. Should anyone think that the new economic entities were simply expanded versions of the old nation-states, playing by the same rules on a larger turf, that hope must quickly be put away. For just as these new markets are contexted and spanned by preexisting global businesses, so also are they enmeshed, and indissolubly linked, by the electronic revolution. The global electronic village is the reality, but what we do in the village marketplace remains to be seen. Transformation is now.

---

[2] It is interesting that the trading floor of the London Market is now closed. The physical manifestation of the market as it used to be is empty and stands as a deserted artifact from another day. Visitors still come to look at it, but nobody does business there any more. Some people have suggested turning it into a restaurant or museum.

CHAPTER III

ORGANIZATIONS IN TRANSFORMATION:
GOING CRITICAL, GOING DIFFERENT

The forces for transformation roll on. As the old ways of doing business are placed at risk, an open space is created in which new ways of being in the marketplace come into being. Some, however, will find the challenge of the moment more than they can bear, and seek to deal with the future as they have with the past.

In organizational terms this means that when the fit between corporation and environment is less than comfortable, the tried-and-true answer is to restructure and reorganize. Somewhere, somehow, it is assumed, the perfect structure will be happened upon. Its shape may be circles or squares, matrices or hierarchies, but given time and wisdom, not to mention luck, that structure will come forth. And with reorganization comes a host of other efforts to find a comfortable and workable shape: mergers, acquisitions, down-sizing and redirection.

Such organizational efforts at adaptation appear as a crazy dance. Starting with slow measured steps, they move toward violently oscillating patterns. Centralize, decentralize, go net-work, go authoritarian control, introduce quality circles, get rid of quality circles, encourage employee participation, run it all from the top.

Just when it seems that there is a momentary respite, and "Finally we can get ourselves organized," some new bolt from the blue crashes through. A corporate raider appears on the horizon. The Middle East erupts in chaos, and oil is shut off. Your only product hits number one on the carcinogen list. The market crashes on the day of your big public offering. The Soviets radically reduce troop strength, peace breaks out, and all your business is in defense.

THE GREAT PICTURE SHOW

The experience is not unlike watching an old motion picture which lurches from frame to frame. Things are moving too fast to catch the details in any single frame, but too slowly and erratically to be comfortable with the flow of motion.

Actually, in the "good old days" we didn't have motion pictures at all, but rather a still shot, which was projected on our screen for what seemed like forever. The details and relationships were frozen, and we grew very comfortable with the sameness. Then some bright, young fellow introduced motion as an added attraction. He placed the old slide projector on rapid advance, and we quickly got the idea that motion was involved. Simultaneously, we began to feel jangled and ill, jumping and bouncing from one slide to the next.

This is Chaos

It is small comfort, but probably useful, to know that the pattern (if you can call it that) evidenced here is analogous to that displayed by any open system caught in the midst of violent environmental disturbance. According to Ilya Prigogene, who has spent a lifetime studying such things, the system moves further and further out of equilibrium until it either explodes and dissipates, or "pops" to a new level of complexity and competence, from which it can successfully deal with the emergent environmental realities.[3] The system "turns every which way but loose" (to borrow the title from the old Clint Eastwood movie), trying all conceivable tricks in its bag. Making adjustments, jury-rigging old procedures, desperately attempting to make sense out of a world that has gone crazy. In the end it lies exhausted, and either retires from the field of battle, or realizes that it is not doing something wrong, *it is doing the wrong thing*. You simply can't get there from here. But what are the alternatives?

Getting Up to Speed

The analogy of the motion picture holds some useful clues. Imagine that we are still sitting in the Great Organizational Picture Show, feeling lurched and bounced. A number of us would like to get our hands on that young fellow, and make him go back to showing one picture at a time — slowly. Unfortunately, it turns out that he is hiding out

---

[3] Ilya Prigogene, Order out of Chaos (Bantam New Age Books, 1984).

in the projection booth with the door locked. More than that, he is positively obsessed with the idea of motion, and just won't listen to any suggestions about slower. Suddenly, one of our number has a totally crazy idea. If not slower, how about faster? Contrary to everybody's better judgment, the suggestion is passed under the door, and the diabolical speed freak obliges.

At first it seems that our worst fears are realized. As each frame succeeds its predecessor, at dizzying speed, we are about to "loose it all" in a meaningless blur. Then a most remarkable thing occurs. As our eyes tire, and we loose the ability to grasp each frame in its discreetness, we are left only with the flow of the moving image. And "*voilà*" — the motion picture is born.

Silly tale with a major point. Life in the Great Picture Show is possible only when you get up to speed, give up on the details, and go with the flow. For us, and our organizations, the issue and the strategy is much the same. When the forms and structures of our lives pass with such rapidity as to become a blur, it is essential to make sense out of the blur.

Making sense out of the blur, or getting past the formal structures of our organizations, is made all the more difficult by virtue of the fact that most of us, at least publicly, act as if there were nothing beyond or beneath those forms. When asked to describe our organization, we typically respond by outlining the organization chart and rendering the balance sheet. After all, those two items, in one form or another constitute the so-called, "hard realities" of organizational life. We all know that position is power, and power is money, and both represent the essence of control. After you have dealt with the chart and the balance sheet, what else is there to say? A great deal, it turns out, though most of it doesn't get printed in the business journals.

Is power really position and budget?

Take the whole business of position power. The conventional wisdom says that unless you have your name on the chart at a high level, you simply do not have the power to do anything worthwhile. That is what we *say*. But, should we find ourselves off in a private corner, facing the question, "How do things *really* get done around here?" it turns out that most people never follow the organization chart, and some folks seem totally unaware that it exists. And strange to say, it is often the latter group that gets the most innovative things accomplished. Recently glorified by Tom Peters as the Skunk Works, these are the people who have found that it is infinitely easier to ask for forgiveness than permission. So much for the formal organizational structure.[3]

When it comes to the balance sheet, and the so-called "hard numbers" of the bottom line, the official position is much the same. It is not just the most important thing, it is the only thing. After all, it is something you can count, count on, and control. This said, we might just remember the events of October 19, 1987. On that day we all discovered that money was only what you thought it was, and we thought it was a lot

---

[3] My point is not that structure is non-useful, it is just not <u>the only</u> thing, nor the most important thing. However, <u>appropriate</u> organizational structure is essential. Please see Chapter X.

less on the 20th than it had been on the 18th. In the United States, we literally dis-imagined half a trillion dollars in 24 hours. It just went <u>poof</u>. So while it remains true that balance sheets are important, and certainly something that you can count, it is not necessarily true that they can be counted on to accurately reflect value. Something else is involved, which is the activity of the "valuer." That is us. When we value things, it is unfortunate but true that our judgment is inevitably subjective. So much for the hard, objective numbers.

It might be said, quite fairly, that I have treated the formal, structural aspects of organizational life with less than due seriousness. But I submit that my treatment of these venerable realities is less severe than the treatment they receive at the hands of the world at large. No comments on my part can possibly place organizational structures in a more tenuous position than the transforming conditions of the world. Like it or not, the organization chart is definitely in the category of, "here today and gone tomorrow."

Likewise with the balance sheet. Obviously every organization needs one, but its hardness and objectivity surely must be suspect in the wake of October 19 and similar events.

The point, however, is not to ridicule these organizational necessities, but rather to place them in perspective. As important as they both may be, there are other elements, or realities, in organizational life of equal or greater importance.

POWER IN THE "SOFT SIDE"

Let us suppose, for the moment, that the official position was wrong, and that in fact the back corridor conversations had some substance. Thus, the keys to leadership, power and organizational effectiveness may not lie exclusively, or maybe even primarily, along the lines of formal position and communication, but rather in that wispy area sometimes referred to as the "informal organization," the soft side of things. A shocking suggestion perhaps, and one which many might rather overlook, if only because it drives directly toward a very sensitive area. The critical issue is *control*, what is it, and do we really have it. And, of course, without control, leadership is impossible, at least according to the Old Story.

The informal organization appears unmanageable. It always seems to be beyond our control, and therefore we suppress it at best, or even totally ignore it. But should it turn out that control, as we have come to understand it, is rather like the emperor's clothes (there only because we desperately wish them to be so), then we might want to take another look at the "informal system." I am reminded of a story about running down Mount Tamalpias.[4]

---

[4] This story is not mine, and could I remember the teller, I would surely credit him or her. It is one of my favorites.

21

Mount Tamalpias

Tamalpias is the majestic peak lying just across the
Golden Gate Bridge from San Francisco. Its upper slopes are
one vast meadowland spilling down to the sea. Given a sunny
day with the wind in your face, resisting the call to run down
the hill is impossible.

On such a day, a young family picnicked at the top, and
when they had finished their meal, the open slopes beckoned.
At first they ran in circles, enjoying the grass, each other, and
the soft earth beneath their feet. But as they ran their random
patterns, they coalesced into a joyful group, bounding down
the hillside. The wind blew their hair, and the steepness of the
hillside striped away all effort. Intoxicated by a feeling of virtual
free fall, they cast caution to the winds and raced downwards.
Feet and legs pumped faster than anybody could remember,
and the exhilarating joy was something none would ever forget.

Suddenly, a collective thought. Their carefree descent
was nothing short of mad. There were rocks in that field, and
trees at the bottom. One misstep and delirious joy would
quickly turn to tragedy.

The immediate response was to stop, but they were well
past the point of no return. To stop at that speed was to court
disaster. If stopping was impossible, careful foot placement
became a necessity. Avoid the rocks, and tufts of grass, the
gopher holes and other secret hideaways of small animals.

Thoughts of care were right, but also impossible. The
speed of descent, to say nothing of eyes filled with windborn
tears, brought vision and thinking to near zero levels. The
choice was obvious, there was no choice at all. They were out

22

of control, and any attempt to regain control could only result in disaster.

The story ended happily, for the family made it to the bottom of the field. They had learned a little something about the siren call of Mount Tamalpias, but more than that, they knew that being in control was letting go.

I suggest that we are all running down Mount Tamalpias. Some of us still think we can stop, or possibly reconfigure the shape of the mountain (create a level playing field). Others run in absolute terror, sustained only in the hope that the bottom will be reached, and the mad flight will come to an end. A few are beginning to suspect that there is no end, and further, that human fulfillment lies not in getting the race over but in running it well.

This latter group contains those strange individuals who had the audacity to propose fixing chaos in the Big Picture Show with more chaos. Speed up, they said, and they were right. Contrary to the conventional wisdom, and counter-intuitive as it might have seemed, sense emerged from nonsense when the discrete bits and pieces disappeared in the blur, and meaning emerged in the flow.

Perhaps order and chaos are not opposites, but necessary, and complementary parts of a continuum, descriptive of the flow of life towards whatever it is about to become. And control is more a matter of letting go. Of course, if the leader is always expected to be in control, it is small wonder that leadership is in trouble at the moment. But that is not, as I have said, the only story.

CHAPTER IV

A WHOLE NEW BALL GAME:
LEADERSHIP AND THE INFORMAL
ORGANIZATION

For people nurtured in the business school environment, who came of age in traditional western organizations, the world of the informal organization appears strange indeed. It is counter-intuitive and somehow wrong. Even though these same people may admit privately that not much gets done in their organization following the old organizational chart, this admission often takes on the aspect of a secret confession. For everybody knows that position is power, and the balance sheet rules. That is what it says in all the books, and of course it must be right.

As a matter of fact, the shadow world of the informal organization is often treated as the enemy. After all, it operates like the underground economy, off the books and beyond the control of those who think (or hope) that they are in control. Given the training and predispositions of many managers, the predictable, primary response to this strange beast is to stamp it out and/or bring it under control. Informal communication, for example, is presumed to be bad, and therefore the Formal Reporting Structure must be adhered to and enforced. The anticipated alternative is chaos.

Failing control, the next strategy is to downplay the power of this "off the books" way of doing business. And so when the academicians and pundits write books on organizations, 99.9 percent (a very rough figure) of what they have to say relates to the observable control functions. The informal organization, if mentioned at all, appears only in a footnote.

The last strategy is to ignore the shadow world completely. By pretending that it just doesn't exist, the notion of formal control is not disturbed.

Given responses such as these, it is not surprising that little is known (officially) about the informal organization, and less use is made of its possible virtues. In more predictable days, when the formal structures apparently worked quite well, the treatment of the informal side of things was not only understandable, but probably justified. Things have changed, and it is time to take a closer look at what is going on underneath the official surface of our organizations, not with the idea of stamping out this strange presence, but rather to learn how it works, and how to use it more effectively.

As a matter of fact, there is a considerable body of experience with the informal side of things, developed over the years by people who were denied access to the formal structures of power. This includes all disenfranchised groups, particularly minorities and women. It also includes people who have chosen to work in the volunteer sector, where the coin of the realm is usually not money and position power, but passion, commitment, and purpose.

> **It may well turn out that the disadvantaged and the do gooders of the world have much to teach those who think they are in charge.**

NEW RULES FOR A NEW BALL GAME

The world of the informal organization is a whole new ball game. But what makes it difficult to adjust to is that it rather *looks* like the old ball game. After all, it is the same world, the same organizations and the same products and services. But appearances can be deceiving.

The relationship between the formal and informal organization, and the difficulties created by the *apparent* sameness of the two are not unlike the relationship between football and football. Same words, but in different contexts they have radically different meanings. In the United States, football is Football. Americans know what everybody else plays is only soccer. The rest of the world has a rather different understanding.

The real difficulty for Americans comes about not just because of the differences, but because of the similarities: same name, same general size and configuration of the field, roughly 100 yards long with goals at both ends. The fans and the teams sit in the same places along the sides, and at a quick glance the pattern of play seems rather similar. Of course, the ball does look a little odd. However, were you to get into a soccer game with the rules of Football still in mind, you would be in "deep tapioca" for sure.

Take the whole question of leadership and who's in charge. In American football, command is exercised from the sidelines by the coach, who transmits the plays to the quarterback via the tight end. How different it is with soccer. *Whoever has the ball is leader.*

There is a strange corollary to the first leadership rule of soccer: *Ball hogs die.* It is absolutely impossible that one person should lead with the ball all the time. When you are playing a nonstop, forty minute half, human physiology, no matter what the level of will and determination, simply will not permit a continuous effort on the part of a single person. And should some person be crazy enough to try such a herculean effort, the net result will be not only total exhaustion for the individual, but also defeat for the team. So much for one, powerful leader.

Speaking of power, much official wisdom suggests that when some obstacle presents itself, the best, and some would say the only, way to victory is to concentrate all available forces, and charge through. Strategy like that may work in American football, but in soccer it is largely ineffective, and generally subject to a penalty call. The basic rule is, *Never oppose force with force.* This does not mean that speed, endurance, and best effort are of no account, but simply that it

27

is much smarter to create a strategy that plays to the weak points and depends on speed and deception for effectiveness.

In order to mount such a non-force strategy, several other rules must be observed. The first is *Play the whole field*. It is, of course, tempting to concentrate only on that which is in front of you. After all, everybody can clearly see the goal at the end of the field. But doing that means that there is only one right way to go — ahead. However, if the way is blocked, and one is observing the cardinal principle of *Not opposing force with force*, it is often necessary to move backward in order to make progress. Thereupon arises the strange phenomenon of watching a team kicking the ball back into its own territory. The intuitive American response is to yell, "Stop, the goal lies ahead!" True, but in order to get there, one has to take maximum advantage of available space in order to reset the dynamics of play and create an open space which reveals the path.

The requirement to sense the dynamics of play, in order to be able to change it, brings to light yet another apparently counter-intuitive principle; it is necessary to *Cooperate in order to compete*. One can not stand removed in abstract isolation and effectively monitor the dynamics of play. It is more like a dance in which the partners must mirror each other's moves before anything else can happen.

Along with cooperation comes one more strange element of relatedness: *Honor the opposition*. Somewhere along the line it became popular to equate the desire to compete and win with high levels of hostility and anger. It is true that occasionally these emotions can produce momentary bursts of superhuman effort, but they are momentary, and for a game of any duration, this is simply insufficient.

> *The New Rules*
>
> *Whoever Has the Ball is Leader.*
> *Ball Hogs Die.*
> *Never Oppose Force with Force.*
> *Play the Whole Field.*
> *Cooperate in Order to Compete.*
> *Honor the Opposition.*

THE BIG BALL GAME

Analogies of all sorts, and sports analogies in particular, are useful only to a point. The short excursion into the world of soccer/football has made clearer some of the ways the informal organizational world differs, but this analogy is limited. Games, by whatever name, are played under narrowly circumscribed conditions: a field of a certain size, with a set number of players, for an agreed upon length of time. Obviously, the world at large doesn't work that way. In the Big Ball Game, the number of players, size of the field, and length of play are constantly changing. Indeed the object of play (what it means to win) is not only up for discussion, it is often several different things at the same time.

Working in the World of 1992, the Global Corporation, and the Electronic Revolution is effectively working in a world of indeterminacy. Anything can change at any time, and usually does. Under the circumstances, it is not surprising that we often make the effort to cut the odds in our favor, and define, albeit arbitrarily, some smaller subset of that total world in which we can set the rules, and thereby gain control. Indeed, that is exactly what we have done with all our games and our businesses. To date, this strategy has been reasonably successful, but its success should not blind us to the fact that it is a strategy, and an arbitrary one at that. We confuse, at our peril, the world of our imagination and the world as it is.

As much as we might wish it were not so, the simple truth of the matter is, *none of us ultimately set the rules*. This is true for the man in the street as well as those elevated individuals we sometimes refer to as our leaders.

For understandable reasons it is comforting to ascribe to The Great Leader the power that we don't have, believing, if only for the moment, that while we cannot control our destiny, He or She can. Truly great leaders understand that ascription of power to be a fond hope, and that they, along with everybody else, are basically out of control. Sometimes, of course, the so-called leaders believe their own press, at which point we are all truly in trouble.

At this juncture, we can certainly benefit from the experience of those who by force of circumstance or choice, have always known that they live in a world which they do not, and cannot, control. For lifetimes and centuries, they have had to play by somebody else's rules.

CHAPTER V

LEADERSHIP LESSONS FROM THE
DISENFRANCHISED:
WOMEN

The prototypical disenfranchised group is women. For whatever reasons, and we are now beginning to understand some of them, women have been seen by men, and often by themselves, as being on the fringes, and certainly not in charge.

> Making generalizations about women, particularly if you happen to be a man, is dangerous. And so it is essential to clarify the basis from which I speak, and my perceived right for doing so.
>
> I speak as a man observing women in my part of the world. That my observations may be warped and biased is a given. As for my right to speak, I take it as true that all humans are both masculine and feminine. As I have come to explore and appreciate my own feminine aspect, I find that disenfranchised woman is not simply a phenomenon of the external world. She exists in me.

The stereotypical view of women, as I was growing up, is captured exquisitely in the song from *My Fair Lady*, where Henry Higgins, the archetype of all male chauvinists, wonders "Why can't a woman be more like a man?" Women, it seemed, were bereft of logic, and were incapable of making plans, or following them through. To the extent that they had a use at all, except as a playthings for men, it was probably to be mothers and caretakers of children. Men, after all, were in charge of the world, and the girls were to be left to girlish things.

How we got to the sorry state represented by the stereotype, is something for the psychologists and anthropologists to puzzle through.[5] But that we were there, and still are in many ways, seems beyond dispute. Given such a view of woman, the resulting depravation and sheer loss of available human potential is inevitable, and nothing short of catastrophic. Fortunately, there seems to be something of a turn. But turn or not, the truly amazing fact remains that, even at a point when the stereotype held its greatest power, women, or at least some women, managed quite well in the world. How they did that is the point of interest.

To the best of my knowledge, the definitive study of effective female strategies under the conditions of radical disenfranchisement has yet to be undertaken. When it is done, I think we will learn that not only did a remarkable group of women accomplish incredible things, but also, and most important for our present situation, we (by which I mean everybody in this transforming world) have a lot to learn from

---

[5] See especially Edward Whitmont, <u>Return of the Goddess</u> (Crossroad, 1982).

their efforts and strategies. Failing such a definitive study, I must rely on what some might term anecdotal evidence, a lifelong, close encounter with a most remarkable group of women: my mother and her friends.

MOTHER AND HER FRIENDS

Mother was born at the turn of the century, into a world that was anything but hospitable to a bright, precocious, young female. Going to school was allowed, but nobody expected it to amount to much, except as it might better prepare a young lady to assume her proper place in life, as the wife of a proper gentleman. College, or anything beyond that was, generally speaking, simply not done.

Mother, it seemed, hadn't read the rule book. Not only did she go to college, but continued on for a graduate degree in English. Degrees in hand, she set forth for the world of work, eventually landing a job with a large New York publisher as an assistant editor. Her authors ranked among the best known of the time, and from the little that I know, she was respected in her work, and enjoyed it immensely.

Then for reasons unknown, she left that world and followed a path much more to the liking of those who judge such things. She got married. How or why all of that came to be, I haven't a clue. I do know that Mother's relationship to my father lasted only long enough for my conception and birth. And then she was on her own again.

Being on her own was not to be equated with being alone, for in fact she had a large circle of women friends, and I suppose some men friends as well, although they were never much in evidence. Mother and her friends maintained close contact year around, but the center of their relatedness was in Maine, where she and I spent all our summers.

Mother's Maine house was her special world, populated exclusively by women. Although it was a strange world for a small boy to grow up in, it was fascinating in a variety of ways, most of which were related to Mother's friends and guests. Over the summers there was a succession of extraordinary women: concert pianists, world class athletes, folks from the world of business and academe. The conversation was civil and urbane, often joyful, and sometimes rational to a fault. And for sure, it bore no relationship to the stereotypical image of the empty-headed woman lamented by Henry Higgins. It seemed idyllic to me then, and in retrospect it appears as a feminine retreat, an isolated place and time where being female was no disadvantage.

Maine was a special place, but more interesting for our present discussions were mother's operations in the larger world. Although she never returned to work in a traditional sense, she was not without a lengthy list of good things to be done: Red Cross drives to organize, blood donor campaigns, fund raising events for the symphony orchestra, and the church. Actually, in order of priority, it was the church and a few other things. Like many women before her and since, Mother discovered the church as a place where she could use her considerable talents. But unlike a lot of those women, she refused to remain in that narrow area known as woman's work.

In fact, she demonstrated a disconcerting tendency for showing up in any number of places clearly labeled Men Only, particularly the Vestry.

The Vestry is the governing body of the local Episcopal Church, and for as long as anybody could remember, The Vestry was the private preserve of men, so much so that Vestry, and Vestrymen, were synonymous. Mother changed all that. She became the first Vestryperson.

I had many opportunities to watch Mother in operation, but how she did what she did, as well as she did, remained a mystery to me for some time. There was no question that she was effective, and that the things she set her sights on largely came to pass, but how she pulled it all off escaped me.

In conversation with her male peers and colleagues, it sometimes seemed to me that she had totally lost her capacity for reason. She would begin with one point, leap to another, fall into inexplicable silence, only to re-emerge from a totally unpredictable, and apparently unrelated, quarter. At times, she appeared the quintessential scatterbrained woman. Yet I knew this lady to be the same one who could pursue a topic with single-minded rationality amongst her friends in Maine. But, what I first took to be an obvious lapse of sense, later emerged as careful strategy. Mother knew what she was doing.

> **Mother set the agenda, bound field, neutralized the opposition, galvanized support, and tied the knot.**

36

While she was never afraid to lead, in the traditional sense of that word, she also had a clear sense of her own limitations and endurance. Practically this meant that she was constantly identifying co-leaders, and incessantly passing the ball off to them. Just about the time the opposition (which was usually male) figured out who the leader really was, all that would change.

What I took to be scatter-shot thinking turned out to be Mother's way of playing the whole field. Although she was quite capable of going to the heart of an argument, she would rarely take the route of frontal assault. Rather she would bounce ideas and comments all around the periphery until she had defined the field she wanted to play on, and contexted it to her liking. Only then would she start to draw the knot.

As a strategy, it was marvelous. Those who opposed her rarely knew where she was going until she got there, and then it was too late. Not only was the die cast by that time, but more often than not, the opposition was thoroughly neutralized. Never opposing the other side directly gave Mother the space to effect alliances and isolate detractors. She knew all about not opposing force with force.

Above everything else, Mother was a lady. Not that she was just nice or proper, although she was certainly both of these, but rather, she gave deep meaning to the words *honor* and *respect*. No matter what side of an issue you might be on, and particularly if you were on a side opposite to her own, you were treated well. This aspect of Mother's strategy (and character) became obvious in a number of ways, but most particularly when she gave a small party.

Crowds of people and the noisy "party scene" were not Mother's cup of tea. But for friends, and especially for colleagues when she wanted to get something done, a small gathering, informally but exquisitely architected, was the chosen field of play. No speeches, no dramatic appeals to recalcitrant opponents' "better nature," nor charismatic summoning of the troops. Just infinite attention to the details of making guests feel comfortable, honored, and respected.

As a witness, and sometime butler, to such occasions, I confess to a certain mystification as to how it all worked. A quiet word here, a fresh drink there, gentle corralling of complementary conversationalists into an off-eddy of the party's flow. Mother didn't like to dance, but she surely knew how to effect the magical movement of genuine communication. Call it what you will, I can only call it leadership.

A son's remembrances of his mother can scarcely qualify as objective reporting, and yet I have seen the patterns and approaches manifest by my mother, practiced by other ladies of a certain age. Too old to be part of, and possibly comfortable with, the women's movement of recent years, and too young to have participated in the suffragette marches, they nonetheless evidenced a style, and power, of leadership from which I think we can learn much. On the outside of power, they held enormous power to effect the changes they held to be important. Their mode of operation was not the standard pattern. They gained power by giving it away, competed by cooperating, rarely if ever opposed force with force, played the whole field with an acute sense of the dance, and above all, honored and respected everybody, and most especially their opponents. In a day when confrontational, charismatic, directive leadership is often idolized in its absence, it may well be that its loss is not to be lamented. Useful alternatives are available.

CHAPTER VI

LIFE IN THE UNDERGROUND:
THE BASICS OF LEADERSHIP

Although Mother and her friends might not have liked the image, I think they operated very much in the underground. From the viewpoint of those "in charge," they were definitely off the books, and not in control of the normal levers of power. Despite this, — actually *because* of it — they managed to accomplish much deemed impossible by those who thought they determined the nature of possibility. Leadership in the underground was not without its power, albeit power that manifests itself is some basic, counter-intuitive, not to say mysterious ways.

As we experience the dissolution of the structures and controls by which we have always done business, it may be well to take another look at that elemental world. The return to basics is partially a nostalgic re-visitation of a simpler age, but it is not necessarily bad for all of that, for it may well be that we missed some important things along the way to our future.

On the simplest level, what we discover are the informal organization and the informal communication system. But these discoveries, I think, are only the beginning, and a rather superficial one at that. Under normal circumstances, the informal system is understood to be more primitive, less sophisticated and evolved. There is a sense in which we have intentionally, and thankfully, left the informal way of doing business behind in our ascent to the present rational mode. The informal system is "less," and the formal system is "more."

In truth, the history of organization, as indeed the history of the species, would seem to justify such a view. There was a time when all of us were hunters and gathers, operating in a very loose and informal set of relationships. However, as we matured, we settled down to create villages and marketplaces. We got "organized."

Businesses follow a similar developmental pattern. Once upon a time in every business, the entrepreneur walked the land: primal, exciting, but basically disorganized. Then there came a day when rational management emerged to straighten out the mess. Stephen Jobs was replaced by John Scully at Apple Computer, for example, and entrepreneurial zeal gave way to Scientific Management. The System is born.

Each stage of organizational evolution[6] has its own style of leadership. The entrepreneurial leader is heavy on charisma, challenge and pure, raw energy. The leader of Rational Business is heavy on structure, control, and logical decision making. Presumably one is an advance over the other, for after all the system works — or so it seemed.

But what happens when the system doesn't work? Obviously we fix the system. And when we run out of fixes, as

---

[6] I owe my colleague Ronnie Lessem a debt of gratitude for showing me these stages of organizational evolution and their leadership styles. He has described them much more completely in his book <u>Global Business</u> (Prentice Hall International, 1989).

41

we seem to be doing at the moment? Again the answer seems obvious, return to an earlier state; we all must become entrepreneurs again, or possibly *intrepreneurs*, in the current jargon.[7]

But maybe, just maybe, our understanding of the entrepreneur and the entrepreneurial organization as a "lower" form of life was correct. And while the entrepreneur possesses many useful and exciting characteristics, such as innovation and high spirits, most of which seem sadly lacking in the increasingly drab world of the organizational system, it may also be true that you can never really go home again. After all, we have certainly had our entrepreneurs in recent days, but as romantic as the cowboys of the business world appear, in fact, the days of the Wild West are over. And so John Scully replaces Steve Jobs. Are we then condemned to oscillate between the entrepreneur and the rational manager/leader, recognizing the insufficiencies of each, but being unable to find anything new?

The problem, I suggest, is that we have been seeking salvation in terms of what we know, while refusing the more profitable, albeit dangerous, journey to the unknown, down to true basics, into the underground. We are right in our assessment of the limitations of the entrepreneur. And unfortunately, our emerging judgment about the rational manager, the leader who runs the System, is also correct. The future resides with neither. It lies deeper than that.

A true journey into the underground is not to be undertaken lightly, for once there we must confront a number

---

[7] *Intrepreneur* is the invention of Gifford Pinchot, and refers to entrepreneurs who work inside a company.

of realities we would just as soon miss. It is not for nothing that we have attempted to construct a rational world in which the churning, chthonic forces, lying beneath the surface of any human organization, are controlled. Pure, raw human energy or Spirit may be awesome and exciting, but it does tend to make a mess. We might start our journey with a story.

THE DRAGON'S TALE

Once upon a time, back when the world was new and all, the Dragon lived in the deep. Known to the Israelites as T'hom and the Babylonians as Tiamat, the Dragon was mother of all, a dark force whose dominion spread from shore to shore. In passion, her awesome power shaped and sculpted the land; a cliff of granite destroyed, a dazzling white beach created. Islands and lagoons, sand bars and channels emerged in response to her restless movement. But with her smile, the seas rippled in delight. Dancing sunbeams made diamonds in the waves, and gentle swells, resonating to her pleasure, caressed the shores of a thousand lands, sending warm tides surging through quiet wetlands, the swampy nursery of all living things.

Then one day, by means now lost in the mists of time, the Dragon was lured from the sea, and banished to a cave. For reasons which seemed good at the time, it was decided by the Powers-that-Were, to put an end to the restless destruction and creation of the Dragon. Too many towns had found their waterfronts endangered, and islanders had grown tired of losing treasured beaches to the Dragon's playful sport. It was bad for business and bad for the tourists. So something had to be done, and off to the cave she went.

As things turned out, the sea is still roiled by the children of the Dragon, but the Dragon passes sunless days confined to the Stygian gloom. The ripples no longer mirror her smile, the swells do not resonate to her pleasure. Should despair and anger drive the Dragon to leave her gloomy abode, the way is blocked by a guard at the gate. St. George by name, this fabled knight stands watch with sharpened sword and stout spear, keeping the Dragon under control.

Once, it is said, the Dragon broke loose while St. George was off on a coffee break. In the twinkling of an eye, the gates were passed and the violent passion, compressed in the cave, poured out across the land. The destruction was truly awesome. Whole villages disappeared in sheets of flame, and castles were tumbled into their motes. For days the Dragon raged until St. George, and a hastily assembled band of junior knights, corralled the beast.

From that day until this, the Dragon has been contained. It is said that the earth trembles with her rage, but very few know the place, and fewer still dare visit. Those who do stand far off, protected by the might of St. George, whispering tales of the day the Dragon broke free.

Quite recently, however, a strange, heretical thought has appeared in the land. What if the Dragon were not the terrible beast so horrendously described in song and fable? Angry for sure, but wouldn't you be angry had you been locked in a cave for millennia? Perhaps the Dragon is only lonely? What would it mean to make friends with the Dragon?

LEADERSHIP IS MAKING FRIENDS WITH THE DRAGON

The Dragon, in forms almost too numerous to count, has appeared as a common element in the imagination and mythology of humankind. The way the Dragon has been treated, however, differs widely around the world. In the West, (including the ancient Near East from which much of the Western tradition has emerged) the Dragon is an awesome beast, as in our tale. Fear is the common response to the Dragon, and much knightly valor has been dedicated to keeping the beast at bay, and under control.

In the Far East, on the other hand, reaction to the Dragon is strikingly different, although the basic image remains remarkably the same. In China and Japan the Dragon is also an awesome beast, surrounded by smoke and fire, and inhabiting the underground. But reaction to the Dragon is the exact opposite of the West's controlling approach. One must learn to respect the Dragon and learn to live with it. In lighter moments, for example during the New Year's celebration, one will dance with the Dragon. And in truth, nothing of import can go on until the Dragon dances.

The Dragon, in all of its manifestations, points to the world of deep, primal power, the surging world of Spirit from which everything, so goes the story, emerges. In the West, the effort is to control, to channel, to render harmless. In the East the effort is toward alignment, seeking to intuit the flow, and move with it. For the West, life with the Dragon represents struggle and conflict. And the hero — may we say leader — is the one who does both best. In the East, life with the Dragon ideally is harmonious, and the leader is the one who shows the way.

Who knows whether Dragons live. In a very real sense, it doesn't make any difference, for it is certain that Dragons existed, and continue to exist, in our minds' images. To the extent that the pictures we hold in our minds tell us something useful about who we are, and who we might become, our Western perception of the Dragon suggests that we are very uncomfortable with deep, surging forces that lie beyond our control.

That insight, if such it be, might best be left on the analyst's couch except for the fact that we apparently have a number of Dragons loose in our world at the moment, none of which we seem likely to control. Might it not be that there is some wisdom from the East? Would it not be well to make friends with the Dragon?

The Yin and the Yang of leadership

Making friends with the Dragon is not to be undertaken lightly, nor should it be confused with what we might call "becoming good buddies." The powers represented by the Dragon are real, awesome, and truly beyond our control. Those who presume to assert control, in the sense we in the West commonly mean, will discover either that the Dragon simply hides out (Spirit disappears), or explodes. Neither result is useful. By the same token, efforts to trivialize (being good buddies), are productive of nasty surprises. At precisely the moment when we think we have it all together, things get out of hand. Making friends with the Dragon requires a strong sense of *balance* and *appropriateness*, which is where the notion of Yin and Yang becomes very useful.

The Eastern notion of *Yin and Yang* describes the conditions under which friendship may be developed and leadership exercised. In the first instance, Yin and Yang are the *balance of opposites*: masculine and feminine, light and dark, order and disorder, chaos and cosmos.

Yin and Yang are inherently paradoxical, and many of us in the West do not like paradoxes. Indeed, when we confront such things, something in our mental apparatus says, "contradiction." From there we proceed to decide which element of the paradox is "wrong." Our rule of thumb is "either/or" — either male or female, light or dark, order or disorder.

Much of the rest of the world looks at the same information, and concludes "both/and." It is always a question of balance. More than balance, it is *necessary polarity*. The light illuminates *only* in the darkness. Order becomes manifest *only* out of disorder, female assumes meaning *only* in relationship to male. And *vice versa* in all cases. There is no right or wrong, better or worse. Always there is both/and.

For leadership, the polarities of Yin and Yang indicate the range of opportunity, the definition of the field on which leadership will be exercised. It is a large field and a broad range. Anything less will restrict the opportunities for growth. Thus, when the world is seen only in masculine terms, the feminine aspects of warmth, nurture, acceptance, caring, and support tend to disappear. But were the situation reversed, so that only the feminine was apparent, the necessary masculine elements of challenge, thrust, judgment, and distinction would be lost. Challenge, left unbalanced by caring is destructive, but acceptance, without critical judgment is mush.

What is true of the polarities of male and female is equally true for order and disorder. Leadership which perceives *order* (cosmos) as its mission, and *disorder* (chaos) as the enemy, will totally miss the opportunities present when the established forms and structures fall away, allowing for the creation of new and more appropriate ones. Such leadership will spend its time holding on to what *was* (order), instead of nurturing the growing edge appearing in chaos. There is no question that chaos is a mess, but messes, like swamps, turn out to be the nutrient feedbed of emergent life.

Our (Western) inability to hold the polarities and accept the paradox of Yin and Yang has led to extremes of leadership style which at best are amusing, and at worst, horribly destructive. When leadership operates exclusively in the masculine aspect, the single "powerful one" takes charge from the top. Decisions are made, but few care to follow because there is no ownership. When leadership swings to the opposite side, and the feminine dominates, "participative management" discusses, and discusses, and discusses. Everybody owns it, but nobody does anything. There is a time for talk, and there is a time to walk. The question is: When and what is *appropriate*?

A sense of appropriateness is critical, but it is also maddeningly elusive. As in poker, you have, "to know when to hold and know when to fold." [8] Should you ask, "When is that?" the usual answer comes back to haunt you — you just have to know. All of which tells us that appropriateness is not a matter of formula. *Three parts participation to one part decision* may look good on the printed page, but it (or any other formulation) simply does not work.

What can not be achieved by formula may be achieved by attention to the flow of Spirit, and continued practice. Just as a champion poker player does not emerge from a single session at the table, and certainly not from a quick reading of the rule book, so in the domain of the Dragon, effective leadership simply does not happen without practice. When the field is known, however, and the cues are recognized by a practiced eye, amazing things can, and do, happen. Spirit will be focused and empowered to get the job done, whatever that job might be. And empowering Spirit is what leadership is all about.

EMPOWERING SPIRIT IS WHAT LEADERSHIP IS ALL ABOUT

---

[8] For non-poker players, it may be useful to know that a central part of the game is bluffing (fooling) your opponents into thinking that you hold better cards than you actually do. If the bluff is successful, the opponents will lay down their cards (fold) in surrender. At which point you win the game. However, if you get caught (somebody "calls your bluff") the tables will be turned. Ergo, "You got to know when to hold and know when to fold."

CHAPTER VII

SPIRIT AND LEADERSHIP

LEADERSHIP IS —
THE CAPACITY TO FOCUS SPIRIT

For many in the West, "Spirit" is nothing.[9] Operating under the premise that if you can't count it, it doesn't exist, the conclusion is that Spirit is not there, or if there, it can't amount to much. At the level of proof there is little, if anything, that can be done to alter this position, for having started with the premise of "countability," the conclusion is inescapable. But, for all the obvious inescapability of the logic, there appears to be a growing sense that the logic utilized need not be the only one. Perhaps it is only the uneasiness of the times, but conversations about Spirit now seem to appear in some of the strangest places. A major corporation, for example, takes out a full page ad to proclaim that a central

---

[9] For example, Edgar Schein writing in Organizational Culture and Leadership (Jossey-Bass, 1985), dispatches the whole notion of Spirit with a parenthetical phrase. He says, "In many cultures, what we would regard as the "Spirit world," *which is not real to us*, would be regarded as extremely real." (Italics added.) My point is not to pick on Schein, but rather to agree with him. In the West, the notion of Spirit typically elicits the sort of treatment Schein gives it.

corporate goal is to "Sustain the Spirit."[10] Perhaps they didn't mean it, but it is interesting that they felt free enough to say something like that.

Of course, there have always been words about Spirit in common conversation, as in "team spirit," "esprit de corps," and the like. But now, somehow, it seems rather more important. A senior executive in the midst of a very nasty takeover battle was overheard to say, "It is remarkable that when everything else is falling apart, we still have our Spirit. If we lose that, I think we have lost everything." I believe he was right. When Spirit disappears, there is not much left.

I have no idea what Spirit is,[11] and for sure I can't show its presence on some dial or gauge. But I rather suspect that the chart displaying the stock market's behavior on October 19, 1987 was a reasonably accurate reflection of the Spirit of the investment community. And if that is so, the connection between Spirit and the bottom line is a direct one.

I take it as a given that Spirit is the most critical element of any organization. With Spirit of the appropriate quantity, quality and direction almost anything is possible. Without Spirit, the simplest task becomes a monumental obstacle. Furthermore, it is in the Domain of Spirit that leadership operates. While it may be true that Leaders have a multitude of very practical tasks, they have one task which outweighs all others, to empower Spirit.

---

[10] The corporation was Shell Canada, and the publication was the program for the Winter Olympics in Calgary 1987.

[11] Readers interested in more on the subject may wish to take a look at my book Spirit: Transformation and Development in Organizations (Abbott Publishing, 1987).

Linking leadership and Spirit presents few problems at the level of casual conversation. Even the popular press has good words to say about "inspiring leadership," and *inspiration*, after all, means "to fill with Spirit." Quarterbacks inspire their teams, generals inspire their troops, presidents are supposed to inspire their companies and countries. That leadership, inspiration and Spirit, all go together seems like a no news item.

The problem is not making the connection, but rather what to do after that. And here again, it appears that the possibility of making a useful, novel statement is limited. University libraries and executive bookshelves are filled to overflowing with innumerable tomes on the subject, ranging from deep studies to shallow nostrums detailing the "Seven Easy Steps to Inspired Leadership." Yet something is missing, either in the literature, its reception, or both.

I think what is missing is a profound sense of the depth of the matter. Leadership is often spoken of as if it were simply advanced management. The presumption is that whatever the manager is supposed to do, the leader does more and better. Leadership is not advanced management, in fact it is radically different from management, and to equate, or confuse, the two is to miss an essential distinction; if observed, it can take us to the heart of the matter.

Before going further, I need to make it exquisitely clear that I am not juxtaposing managers and leaders, rather I am concerned with functions. The truth of the matter is that we all lead and we all manage.

In general, we are quite clear about what managers are supposed to do. They control the system, whatever that system might be. And the operative word is *control*. A good manager makes the plan, manages to the plan, and meets the plan. The details are taken care of, the aberrancies controlled, and the problems solved.

It almost has become popular to denigrate managers, as if they were somehow a lesser breed, and not all that useful. Nothing could be further for the truth. For as long as we have systems that are basically workable in the extant environment, we need managers, very good managers.

In the post World War II years, the manager reigned supreme. Everyone wanted to be a manager, and management, quite rightly, was understood to reside at the top of the heap. Under relatively stable conditions, or conditions where things were changing in a linearly predictable fashion, the role of management is effective. But, when the balance swings to non-stability, and change occurs in radical, discontinuous jumps, the skills of management don't work quite as well as they used to.

The tasks of management and leadership are, I believe, separate and distinct. To manage is to control. To lead is to liberate. To manage is to work at the level of the system. To lead is to work in the depths beneath the system, in the primal areas where the Dragon lives.

> # To manage is to control.
> # To lead is to liberate.

LEADERSHIP IS LIBERATION — BEING OUT OF CONTROL AND LOVING IT

In the everyday world, we take it as a given that when we loose control we are crazy, and indeed there is no small amount of experimental evidence that people with little or no perceived control over their lives are driven crazy.

Craziness, in the Domain of Spirit, is the perception that we *are in control*. The reality is that Spirit moves as it wants, changing shape, form, intensity, and direction with the speed of a whim, and the passage of a mood. Just when you think you've got it, like a wisp of smoke, it passes through your hands to appear in another place, or disappear all together.

Talk like this may seem imprecise, as indeed it is, but the experience alluded to is familiar to all. The coach of an outstanding team knows all to well that having the best players, game plan and coaching staff does not automatically insure the championship. Some days the "guys are hot, and some days they're not." Corporate executives know that while state-of-the-art plant and facilities, matched with skilled workers and managers, are strong cards to hold, the competitive edge is not guaranteed.

At the other extreme are those instances where few of the accoutrements of success are in hand, and yet miraculously, or at least it appears as a miracle, good things happen. In the nick of time, despite all odds, at the last moment, the deal is closed, the game is won, the company is saved. In retrospect, it is always nice to feel that everything was part of the plan. But those who were there, and particularly those who assumed the role of leadership, know differently. If it was a plan, it was surely a different kind of plan, for things turned out in ways that nobody had any right, or reason, to expect. In private moments of honesty, it is often reported that things began to work precisely when all attempts at *making them work* were given up. Being in control, paradoxically, meant being out of control, and going with it. But being out of control does not mean being without principle.

THE FOUR IMMUTABLE PRINCIPLES OF SPIRIT

Spirit plays by its own principles, which from the viewpoint of standard management practice, are not only strange, but aggravating in the extreme. I am not sure, of course, that they are immutable, but they always seem to apply. They are: (1) Whoever comes is the right people, (2) Whatever happens is the only thing that could have, (3) Whenever it starts is the right time, and (4) When it is over, it is over.

The Four Immutable Principles occurred to me originally as a rather facetious way to describe the operative conditions in meetings and conferences. I then discovered that they were no joke, and further, that violating them inevitably produced disastrous results. I admit that it *seems* that the principles suggest a total "just let it happen" approach, prescriptive of failure. To be sure, one must make best effort to get ready. Details of time and space must be attended to. But when all that is done, or done as well as it can be, then the only thing to do is to follow the principles. Like it or not, whoever comes are not only the right people, they are the only ones there, and whatever happens is going to happen with them, or not at all. Recognizing these principles saves untold amounts of anxiety and "might have beens," which can become so overpowering that the real, present opportunities are overlooked. The Immutable Principles work, I believe, in meetings and conferences because they are descriptive of the way that Spirit works.

First Principal — Whoever Comes Is the Right People reminds us that Spirit cannot be forced. In those situations when word has come down from on high that a certain position or initiative is an organizational "must," which requires "spirited participation," there is absolutely no way in the world to insure that all members of the organization will buy in. Seeking such a result not only guarantees failure, it is also the total perversion of what Spirit is all about. Spirit forced is Spirit killed.

The fact that some do not feel inclined to join is no indication of failure unless it is defined as such. However, if the would-be leader will observe the First Principle, there is a high likelihood that not only will the Spirit rise, it will be infinitely deeper and richer than ever could have been imagined. All who choose to participate will do so from, and for, their passion. Their passion provides the essential, powerful source of innovation and performance.

Second Principle — Whatever Happens Is the Only Thing That Could Have reminds us that leadership is not control. That is management. Leadership is rather the creation of a nutrient open space in which genuine human fulfillment may be achieved. The problem is that would-be leaders, for their own reasons of insecurity, often feel they must manage. After all, things could get out of control. The truth of the matter is, not only *can* things get out of control, that is virtually guaranteed to happen, if Spirit is really up and powerful.

This is a difficult point for one who leads. There is an understandable feeling that, having accepted the responsibility of leadership, he or she must also specify exactly how everything will turn out. The understandability of this feeling does not change its negative impact. As all parents understand, or come to understand, giving birth to a child, while creating some proprietary interests, is not licence to specify outcome. To forget this is to invite rebellion or withdrawal. The same is true with Spirit.

Third Principle — Whenever It Starts Is the Right Time. In a curious and important way, Spirit exists out of time. Indeed Spirit creates time. For Westerners driven by the clock, this is difficult to deal with, but the rest of the world understands that truly important events always make their own time. Actually, we in the West understand this too. We say, without thinking about it, that the current year is 1989 A.D. We tend to overlook that this dating has meaning only in the context of a particular manifestation of Spirit. It is, after all, 1,989 years after the birth of Jesus of Nazareth. No matter what we, as

57

individuals, may think about that particular person, there is no question that even the Western time system is Spirit based. Of course, if Spirit is manifest in a different person or place, you have a different time. Thus for the Jews, it is well into the fifth millennium; for the Hindus, the birth of Vishnu, some 4,000 years ago, is central.

When Spirit appears, it doesn't happen according to the clock. Whenever it happens is not only the right time, but its own time. Needless-to-say, senior executives hoping to raise the Spirit of a place find this principle annoying, but that doesn't change its power. The emergence of Spirit, will inevitably frustrate the keepers of the corporate calendar.

Fourth Principle — When It's Over, It's Over. The manifestation of Spirit as all things appearing in time and space has a lifespan, and when it is over, it is over. Certainly Spirit may be renewed, or sustained, but there comes a time when its particular form simply runs out of steam.

The Four Immutable Principles

- Whoever comes is the right people.
- Whatever happens is the only thing that could have.
- Whenever it starts is the right time.
- When it is over, it is over.

CHAPTER VIII

THE FUNCTIONS OF LEADERSHIP

The central task of leadership is to liberate and focus Spirit, guided by the Four Immutable Principles. In practice, however, there are some rather more specific functions of leadership, which we will examine here and in the following chapters.

The Five Functions
of
Leadership

To Evoke Spirit with Vision.
To Grow Spirit by Collective Story Telling.
To Sustain Spirit with Structure.
To Comfort Spirit at the End.
To Revive Spirit when Grief Works.

VISION — THE EVOCATION OF SPIRIT

Leadership in not a matter of command and control. It is the evocation and alignment of Spirit. Spirit cannot be commanded, it may be invited. Spirit cannot be coerced, it may be channeled. Spirit rarely, if ever, responds to answers, but rather questions, which create the nutrient Open Space in which it may flow. Vision poses the question that creates the space into which Spirit flows, and becomes powerful.

It has become popular for organizations to engage in "visioning," the end product of which is a vision statement. The advent of visioning as a legitimate corporate practice is certainly to be applauded, for it recognizes precisely the realities we are discussing. But the equation of vision with a vision statement is at best weak, and at worst, a total perversion of what vision is all about.

There is an acid test for the effectiveness of vision statements. One simply posts them on the wall and asks the group involved, "Would you be willing to die for that?" If the answer is no, there is reasonable indication that the statement is only words, untouched by the power of vision.

Upon examination, it usually turns out that such ineffective vision statements emerge in one of two ways. Usually, they are the product of the titular leader's description of what the business is all about, issued very much in the style of a policy directive. Alternatively, the vision statement comes √ into being after endless hours of committee meetings. This is simply a case of the right idea done in the wrong way, for

61

vision is not a policy statement, nor the product of a committee. It comes from an entirely different place.

THE GENESIS OF VISION

Vision emerges from the depths. It comes from the Domain of the Dragon (Chapter VI) in ways that contravene logical policy making, or standard committee procedure. The exact mechanics are a matter of current evolving discovery, but they seem to have a lot to do with the powers of intuition and the operation of what now would be called the "right brain." [12] But if the precise mechanics are less than clear, the phenomenon has long been known.

The birthing place of vision is the Open Space created when things fall apart, and difference is perceived. It emerges when an old way of being, or doing things, is no longer appropriate, or effective, and a new one has yet to emerge. The instigating moment may be the end of a particular business or product, the exhaustion of a theoretical concept, or way of looking at things. In extremes, it may be the dissolution of a social order. In all cases, the instigating factor is the awareness of ending.

This moment is far from comfortable, for by definition, all the usual supportive elements defining the way things were

[12] The literature in this area grows geometrically by the year, but for some general reading consult Willis Harman and Howard Rheingold, Higher Creativity (Tarcher, 1984) and also Phillip Goldberg, The Intuitive Edge (Tarcher, 1983).

supposed to happen, cease to exist. Even the stouthearted will experience fear and a sense of emptiness. But emptiness is the clearing in the forest of everyday activities, the Open Space in which vision may emerge.

The good news of Open Space, at the point of ending, is that things can be seen with a degree of clarity that the business of everyday life obscures. When all the schedules, "to do" lists, committee meetings, are over, there arrives a profound and rich moment, in which it is possible to ask what it all means anyhow. Attempts to fill up the Open Space with yesterdays answers are automatic, but futile.

Vision, at its point of genesis, appears in forms most notable for their variety. For some, it is a "still small voice." Einstein apparently *heard* his visions as music, which he later translated into mathematics. In an early stage of the development of my own theory of Spirit, I was struck by a recurrent image of a double-ended vortex. Others report experiencing various colors, shapes, and sounds, made significant only by the inescapable awareness that meaning, unclear and undefined to be sure, was present.

I use the word "inescapable" with intention. Vision is compelling, even compulsive, which is both the problem and the power. Recurrent images (in whatever format) tend to be crazy-making, and those who report such recurrent images are often taken to be crazy. Indeed, the difference between hallucination and emergent vision may be almost imperceptible.

The *power* of vision also derives from this sense of inescapability and compulsion. Visionaries are, typically, driven people. In the vernacular, they see things that others don't see, march to a different drummer, play by new rules. In a word, they tend to be strange and difficult to get along with. Their strangeness or differentness is easy to understand, for by definition, they have perceived, in the Open Space, some difference that makes a difference (to them). Where others see only ending (destruction), or nothing at all, those possessed by the vision see some difference, small or large, that renders futurity a possibility, and marks the first step toward a new version of reality.

If visionaries are compulsive, they are also frustrating, for they tend to talk in repetitive circles, struggling to bring their object of awareness into focus. Their compulsion gives them the appearance of certainty. Their lack of clarity will often make them an object of scorn. It is very difficult to be convinced of something that nobody else can see, and it is just as hard to live with one who suffers from such a conviction. But all of that comes with the territory.

It is more than a little tempting to ask the source of the vision. Strict behavioralists, convinced that human behavior, in all its forms, is simply the outcome of electrochemical reactions, will posit a bad dinner the night before. Neurophysiologists might propose the "right brain." Humanistic psychologists offer the "unconscious mind." And mystics will identify the great cosmic abyss. I don't know. But if pressed, I would suggest, from the Domain of the Dragon, a manifestation of Spirit. Although the question is important, the answer, for our purposes, is not essential. It is only important that vision begins in Open Space with the perception of difference.

SHARING VISION — FROM ONE TO THE MANY

The Cost of Vision Vision, for all its power and potential, is not worth a great deal so long as it remains the private preserve of a single individual. Once shared, however, it has the capacity to focus and galvanize Spirit in remarkable, and often breathtaking ways. The distance, however, from the one to the many is not small, and traversing that distance cannot be done without cost.

One of the best descriptions of the passage of an emergent vision is provided by Thomas Kuhn in his book *The Structure of Scientific Revolutions*.[13] Although Kuhn might not like the suggestion that he is writing about vision, I believe that to be the case. His actual subject matter is the arrival of the different scientific conceptual models, or in his terms, *paradigms*, through which the world is understood.

Stripped to essentials, a paradigm is a way of looking at reality that makes sense; it arises from the end of an older version, with some significant difference perceived. While vision

---

[13] Thomas Kuhn, The Structure of Scientific Revolutions (Chicago, 1970).

may lack some of the scientific precision possessed by paradigm, I take them to be the same.

We learn from Kuhn that the progress of scientific knowledge does not occur in the nice, linear pattern that high school science classes sometimes suggest. It occurs in great, tumultuous leaps, when an older vision proves inadequate. The story is that once upon a time there was a standard way of looking at the world (be it Ptolemaic, Babylonian, Copernican, or Newtonian) which worked quite well, until it was noticed that everything didn't quite fit in. And so the theory was adjusted to fit the anomalies. Its proponents said something like, "The theory is true, except for..." After a while, the exceptions grew greater than the rule, and something had to give. But not without a struggle.

Those who lived by the old world view were loath to change. Things were quite comfortable as they saw it, and dealing with reality in a new way was not quite what they had in mind. At the same time, a small, growing band found the exceptions inescapable, and the rule intolerable, and so they imagined (may we say visioned?) a different way of looking at things.

Heresy! Quite literally. People paid in blood, and often with their lives, for seeing things differently. And those on the "other side," quite understandably, resisted the change. For implicit in the acceptance of change was the acknowledgment of the passage of the old order. Those who had defined their lives in terms of the old order discovered that their lives, as they had always known them, were not only different, but through. Not pleasant.

Pre Vatican II religious life vs post Vatican II religious life

66

GATHERING SPIRIT

Before vision can focus Spirit, it must first gather Spirit. And that is no simple task, especially when the folks involved are not at all sure that the new direction is in their best interest, or that they want to be "gathered." All of which leads to some suggestions on the specifications of effective vision, effective in the sense that it really inspires — or *in-spirits*.

> ## Powerful, effective Visions have three qualities. They are Big, Attractive and Do-able.

The Qualities of Effective Visions

Powerful, effective visions have three qualities. They are Big, Attractive and Do-able. *Big* is not a question of being grandiose, but rather commodious. The vision must be big enough to actually gather all the Spirit inside. Obviously spatial talk is not really appropriate when speaking of Spirit, but it may get the idea across. The point is that the vision must be large enough to provide room, and more, for all the folks who are likely to participate. There must be space for all essential points of view, frames of reference, skills, occupations or whatever. When vision is too small, it is exclusive, and the power of vision to gather Spirit will be vitiated from the start, no matter how good or exciting the vision may be.

Not only must vision be big enough for all the players, as they are at the moment, there must also be plenty of room to grow. *Vision is never an answer, but always a question which initiates a quest towards the fulfillment of the participants.* It is a journey which elicits the best that everybody has, and simultaneously provides the space in which they might become infinitely more than they ever imagined. Certainly a vision must have a focus, just as a journey must have a destination, but when the journey's end is totally known in advance, it is scarcely worthwhile undertaking.

Mystery and awe are experienced in the presence of powerful visions, which also usually means the presence fear. In extremes, fear may prevent some from entering into the vision, and it may well be that they should not go on the journey; but unless the tingle of fear is known somewhere at the beginning, there is a strong likelihood, indeed absolute certainty, that the vision is too small. Tame visions go no where.

The second characteristic of a powerful, effective vision is *Attractiveness*. Spirit cannot be coerced, it must always be invited, and few will accept an unattractive invitation. If vision provides the space for growth, it must also propose an appealing direction for growth. Nobody has to enter into the vision. The test for the individual is always, "Do I want to be like that?"

Last, a powerful, effective vision must be *Do-able*. Do-able has two senses, first that it be technically feasible. There have been lots of big, attractive visions which foundered for the simple reason that there was no way on earth they could be accomplished. Obviously, good visions will, and must, push the limits of technology, but if there is no sense of a likely, positive outcome, the possibility of eliciting a reasonable number of "co-journers" is limited at best.

The second sense of Do-able is "historically possible." There are many visions which are big, attractive, and possess technical feasibility — which are just inappropriate to the circumstances of those addressed. The feeling here is, "That might be somebody else's vision, but not ours."

A very good example of historical non-do-ability, appears in the reaction of non-Western countries to the vision of Western Economic Development. Few citizens of non-Western countries knowledgeable about the Western vision would deny either its bigness or attractiveness, and the technical feasibility has been amply demonstrated. But there remains a real sense that, good though it may be, it is not us. Westerners, of course, have viewed this reaction as being something between madness and idiocy, but it may well turn out that not only were the doubters right in terms of their own history, but also in terms of the history (nature) of the planet. Western technology, as a driving vision, clearly has its limitations, as evidenced by its propensity for fouling the nest we all live in.

One might suspect that having the *Three Criteria for Effective Vision* firmly in hand, it should now be possible to design a vision that would be irresistible. I think that is unlikely, for the simple reason that Spirit doesn't work that way. It is true that Spirit seems to follow certain principles, but they are not mechanistically coercive. More accurately, to the

69

extent that there are mechanics, they are the mechanics of the quantum and not of Newton.

When dealing with things, such as a large rock, Newton tells us that, given a lever of sufficient length and strength, combined with some leverage point, the rock *will* move. Quantum mechanics tells a different story. In the world of high energy, the Principle of Indeterminacy applies. Although it may sound rather odd, this principle says that given enough rocks, levers, and time, some rock, somewhere, will probably move. In a word, with thorough study and careful work, one may raise probability, but never to the level of certainty. Raising probability with vision and Spirit requires that we remember the Four Immutable Principles.

VISION AND THE FOUR IMMUTABLE PRINCIPLES

First Principal — Whoever Comes Is the Right People reminds us that becoming inspired, electrified and turned on by any vision is always a matter of personal choice. A vision forced is a vision killed. Vision, after all, is a question and an invitation to fulfillment.

Second Principle — Whatever Happens Is the Only Thing That Could Have. Visions (like parents) that specify end results in detail are bound to be frustrated. Such visions become limitations and not evocations. Be prepared to be surprised.

Third Principle — Whenever It Starts Is the Right Time. Vision does not occur in time, but rather time occurs in the context of vision. When vision strikes, it creates its own time, and that is one of the ways that we know it was real vision, and not just a flash in the pan.

Fourth Principle — When It's Over, It's Over. Visions have a life span, and when it is over, it is over. Certainly visions may be renewed, or sustained, but there comes a time when a particular vision simply runs out of steam, and its capacity to focus Spirit wanes and ceases. That is true in the record of scientific visions, as the Ptolemaic picture of the universe gave way to Copernicus, from thence to Newton, and on to the quantum theorists. Each, in its own time, created a frame of reference from which to make sense out of what was going on in the world. Then the exceptions appeared and the anomalies grew. It was not that the vision no longer was true, it simply lacked the power to focus Spirit. When it is over, it is over.

CHAPTER IX

THE FUNCTIONS OF LEADERSHIP: GROWING SPIRIT THROUGH COLLECTIVE STORYTELLING

Spirit, evoked by vision, can only begin to realize its potential when the vision is not only shared, but grown. Leadership has a central part to play in this process through Collective Storytelling.

Storytelling may seem a rather weak reed with which to build an organization, but that is to misunderstand the power of stories. When I say *story*, I am not referring to some idle or amusing tale, but rather the central vehicle through which the Spirit of an organization is gathered and focused on the job at hand. The Story is the *organizational mythology*.

Having said myth, I may have made the situation even less comprehensible, for to many myth is not only an idle tale, it is by definition *untrue*. Contrary to this view, myth is neither true nor untrue. Rather, it is *behind* or *beneath* truth; it establishes the context within which people talk to each other, and determine the truth. A short example may clarify.

WHAT'S THE STORY? — THE POWER OF MYTH

Suppose you walk into a business as a prospective employee. You are presumably interested in all the normal, first-line questions dealing with compensation, benefits, job description, hours of operation, organizational structure, all of which are provided to you through a series of tables, charts and manuals. Necessary as that material is, it seems a little dry and abstract. You press deeper to questions that are more amorphous, but very important, questions about working conditions; what it would feel like to work in this place, and what it all really means. Some answers will appear just by walking about and looking at the physical circumstances, the layout of the facility, color on the walls, the patterns of activity, but sooner or later you will find it necessary to identify some kind of context in order to determine what is different about this place from all others. And most important, do you really want to be a part of it?.

At such a moment, it is almost guaranteed that you will search out an individual with whom you feel comfortable, and ask, "What's the story anyhow? What's *really* going on?" Questions such as that are best asked after hours, in a bar, a coffee shop, or over dinner, all far removed from the "official presentations." That is time to get down to where the "rubber meets the road," to the "nitty gritty," in order to hear the "real story."

If you reflect on what you learn then, you may be surprised to find that the "real story" has very little to do with the "cold objective facts," which you probably already knew. "The real story" ends up being closer to war stories.

In a curious way, the facts of the matter don't make any difference, indeed you may have a strong suspicion that the events recounted never happened at all. Regardless, something important is being communicated through what seem to be incidental examples. That "something" is the feeling or meaning of a place, which establishes the context within which all of the bits and pieces of an organization's life start to make sense. Without stretching a point, we might even say that the stories tell us something about the Spirit of a place. In fact, these stories do more than tell about the Spirit of a place, they actually bring us into immediate encounter with that strange thing we call Spirit.

Supposing that in our imaginary conversation over the cup of coffee, the tale goes like this:

> "I don't know what they told you up in the front
> office, but let me tell you like it really is. Last
> week, the boss called in five managers, looked at
> the numbers, and fired the bottom two
> managers. No warning, no separation packages,
> just OUT. I got to tell you, this is a schlock
> outfit. Top management is just out for itself."

No graduate degree in Organizational Psychology is needed to assess the quality of Spirit in the place. And the "fact" that there may have been six managers instead of five, and only one got fired and not two, makes very little difference in that assessment. The story very quickly communicates the reality of Spirit in the place, and it is significant not only in itself, but also in the fact that your confidant chose to tell it to you. Even if the events described never happened, the very telling of the story gives you a fast picture of what is going on.

Now obviously, one story once told does not a myth make. So the next day you go back and casually ask a number of people if they ever heard "the one about," and while the details and numbers vary widely, it becomes obvious that the story is there. Of course you may ask if it is true, but probably by that point it becomes clear that the historical truth or falsehood of the tale is infinitely less important that the fact that it is being told.

Senior management, if confronted with the story, would undoubtedly be upset. Either they would try to downplay it by saying something like, "Aw, that's just a war story," or to discredit it, by giving their version of the "true facts." Neither approach is likely to be very effective, for to see it as just a war story is to overlook the intensity, even passion, with which the tale was told. And giving the "facts" will probably do little more than to elicit a response like, "Well, that's their story."

The point is *that stories are powerful, and they quickly and accurately reflect the Spirit of a place*. Indeed, these stories may be the most powerful element of organizational life, for they create the context within which everything that happens is interpreted. Saying they are of no value, or untrue, does not change their impact, as would quickly become clear were senior management to challenge this power. Should an "official denial," be issued that would be taken as one more example of the duplicity of the top brass.

Even apparently positive efforts to change the story are likely to backfire. Imagine the general reaction were the fired managers suddenly rewarded with a large separation package; a lot of head scratching and wonderment about what "those SOBs are up to now, 'cause the story is...."

The story is, and the story rules, which is why those who would lead must pay special attention to the tales that are told, or could be told. For the Story not only reflects the Spirit of a place, it shapes that Spirit and determines the ways it shall behave.

CREATING THE COLLECTIVE STORY

The driving story of an organization is never just the story of the founder. However, it starts there, for vision is the organizational mythology in future tense. The power and the passion of the primary vision will be sufficient to generate excitement if that vision is big and attractive. And the excitement will be grounded and focused if, and as, the visionary begins to deal with "do-ability," both technical and historical. A reasonable case must be made that the particular vision could be accomplished by those who hear the tale. But the essential shift from excited interest to committed involvement will only take place when the story becomes a collective one. No longer the Founder's tale, but *our* story.

> **Vision is the organizational mythology in future tense.**

Captured imagination is the beginning, but its growth is essential. Inspiring a group of folks to believe in a new idea is always the first step, but letting that idea truly be theirs, to be evolved as they are able and interested, marks the difference between short-term excitement and long-term commitment. From here on out the telling of the tale, even in the future tense, must be a collective activity, and it is exactly here that difficulty emerges. Visionaries, who have passionately given birth to new ideas, often find it difficult to let them go. And letting go is the essence of the operation.

It is an old truism that everybody sees everything from their own perspective, which means that when it comes to storytelling, each must tell it in his or her own way. Thus the marketer's story about the new product will probably have much more to say about the market than the product, while the engineer will tell a tale with exactly the reverse points of emphasis, and so it will go with all the potential participants. The opportunity for misunderstanding, because of differences in language, is acute, but the possibility that offense may be taken by the original visionary is higher.

As the story is told and retold from the several points of view, it will inevitably loose some of its original purity and focus, even as it gains breadth and depth. For the one who conceived the vision, this can be very painful indeed. Leadership here involves resisting offence and maintaining both the Open Space in which the story can be told, and also the focus of the tale, so it makes some sense. In a word, the Second Immutable Principle must be honored. No matter what level of effort, it will remain true that whatever happens is the only thing that could have. Really letting go is essential.

Maintaining Open Space is a job that many will find difficult, for it involves *less* rather than *more*, waiting as opposed to moving. It is so tempting to fill up all the space with meetings and agendas, under the impression that something must be done. But this is to forget that the most fertile ground for the growth of Spirit is a question. The press of business and the passion of the visionary both drive for closure, but if those drives are heeded before all needed participants have an opportunity to contribute, the vision will die stillborn.

In practical detail, the leader must set the direction and manage the boundaries, while leaving almost everything else to the participants themselves. Observably, the leader's sole contributions may be only a few remarks to the effect that, "I think we are in widgets and not whatsits."

The leader also has some work to do inside the boundaries, but that is less telling people what to do and think (lining out the plan), than making the connections and drawing out the implications of the several stories as they are told. It is a given that engineers and marketers, for example, will not understand each other at significant points. Even when they use the same words, they will be used with different meaning. Part of maintaining Open Space is to constantly clear away the obfuscation of jargon. There is no easy way to do this, for every professional group develops its own jargon, and worse than that, presumes that its language makes sense. One almost sure-fire way of reducing jargon is to invite people back to the level of storytelling. Move them away from abstractions, on to a narration of what "it" would look like if everything worked.

LEADERSHIP IN ACTION

A story about leadership in action will make all of this more concrete. Several years ago, Owens Corning Fiberglas (OCF) of Toledo, Ohio, had an unfortunate run in with a small lumber yard on the West Coast by the name of Wicks. At the time, OCF was the dominant force in the fiberglass business. They invented the stuff, and were doing about four billion dollars worth of business each year. Known as Big Pink in the trade, (pink for the color of their product, named in honor of their mascot, the Pink Panther) they set the trends, and seemed secure in their position.

Then the sky fell. Wicks made a hostile run on Big Pink, and when the dust settled, management was still in control, but under very reduced circumstances. In order to pay off the raiders and stockholders, to say nothing of the army of lawyers and accountants, OCF went from having half a billion dollars in the bank to being a billion and a half in the hole. Not a happy time. Businesses were sold, employees terminated, and annual sales moved from four billion to a little over two billion.

The hero of the moment was Max Weber, better known as Max, or Super Max. To hear the stories, Max did everything. He sold the banks on a bailout package, sold businesses to make the terms, and led the troops to safety at enormous cost. Fourteen hour days, seven day weeks were the norm for all those who remained. After six months of this behavior, there was good news and bad news. The good news was that the company had not only survived, but was actually coming out of the woods. The bad news was that all those who had pulled off this miracle were just about Maxed out.

79

I had been working with OCF during this period, and during one session with a cross-section of folks, we were reviewing the state of the OCF Spirit. One word summed it up: dragging. When we got down to the question of what to do about it, I suggested, in almost an offhanded manner, that it would probably be useful to have a "Thank You Max Party," as a way of saying thank you to Max, and all the others, who had put in the long hours, and also to mark a turning point to whatever it was that was to come next. Honoring the past and moving to the future, so to speak.

I had scarcely gotten the words out of my mouth when two young women, almost in unison, said, "We are going to do that." Interestingly enough, they did not say, could we, should we, or may we — but, We are going to do that. It needs to be said that OCF had virtually no female executives, senior or otherwise. The thought that two young women could make such an affirmative statement was fairly astonishing.

Their statement turned out to be the tip of the iceberg. In 48 hours, they, singlehandedly, enlisted the interest and support of 40 plus people from all over corporate headquarters, established the time for a preliminary gathering, and were well on their way to doing something significant. Eight weeks from the day of their declaration, the Thank You Max Party, which by that time had been converted into the *Pink Pride Rally*, took place. Thirteen hundred people in pink t-shirts, drinking pink lemonade, regaled by the Pink Panther under 600 pink balloons gathered beneath a hugh banner which said THANK YOU. For two hours, they celebrated their past and looked for the future.

That the party occurred at all was remarkable, but the way that it came into being was even more surprising. Without formal budget, top-down approval, assigned staff, or any of the other standard necessities of getting things done in corporate America, these two young women made it all happen. Not that there weren't moments of anxiety, not to say imminent disaster. But when zero hour arrived, the show went on.

How did they do it? Quite simply, they had a vision, held the vision, shared the vision, and grew the vision. And the vision became reality.

From the opening meeting until the opening gun, they operated superbly as mistresses of the informal organization. They began by telling a likely story of what it could/would be like, without worrying at the start about all the problems and reasons why it couldn't be done. When the story had grown rich enough so that the imagination of others was hooked, all those interested were invited to grow the collective tale.

At times it seemed like confusion twice confounded, and those with a more orderly streak were sure that nothing concrete would ever happen. But the organizers pressed on. Nobody was told what to do, rather they were invited to contribute their best thoughts and actions.

Some of the suggestions were, by almost any standard, just plain crazy. But when those insane ideas were laid on the table of the organizing group (whose membership changed from meeting to meeting in confirmation of the First Immutable Principle), the proposers were honored, even as the ideas were seen to be a little off the mark. Indeed, it often seemed to be the rule that when a "crazy idea" was rejected, that merely opened the space for two sound ideas to be born.

Case in point was the question of invitations. How do you get folks to come to the party? Standard procedure dictated an approach to the CEO to receive his blessing and signature on an appropriate memo of invitation. The idea was deemed crazy for two reasons. First of all, it was by no means certain that the CEO would approve, and should he be asked, and then disapprove, the whole thing was off. Equally important to the organizers was ownership of the rally. Were the invitation to come from the top, it would then be "their" party. Not bad, but not quite what everybody had in mind. The party, if it were really going to work, would have to be "our" party. Solution? One of the young ladies took herself to the CEO's office and invited him.

relationship proximity network

Nobody had to come, and nobody had to participate, either in the rally itself or in it preparations. But those who did come, came from a point of passion. They had seen the vision, believed they could contribute, and took personal responsibility for making their ideas a reality. As for the young women, they created the nutrient open space in which the Story was grown *collectively*.

The significance of the event went far beyond having a good time, although that certainly took place. During a party to celebrate The Party, folks had an opportunity to tell the story and remember the highs and lows. The stories were told with animation, and often concluded with words such as, "I really felt like I made a contribution, and I have never had so much fun in all the 30 years I have spent in this corporation, nor felt that my contribution was so worthwhile and appreciated." "I really felt that I made a difference, but it was only a party."

When the last comment came by, about it being only a party, I asked: Was it? When was the last time you remember two young woman with no budget, formal authority, or management-selected team putting on a major shindig for 1,300 of your best customers? And did all of that in eight weeks from concept to delivery? I think you have done much more than a party — indeed there is nothing that you have done here which does not have immediate business application. OCF, like many corporations, has hugh social gatherings for customers and clients, which may take a year and a million dollars to put together. The comparison was not only obvious but odious.

Some other ground had been broken too. The great myth of powerlessness had, in principle, been laid to rest. If two young women, one an accountant and the other a secretary, could do what they did, nobody, ever again, could say, "I can't do that because I don't have the position power." There may, of course, be *many good* reasons not to do something, (not appropriate, fear of punishment, and so on), but they are all good reasons and not *sufficient* ones. The power to make a difference is there if you choose to use it.

Last but by no means least, is the issue of leadership. The case can be made that, certainly during the hours of the rally, and those immediately preceding it, corporate leadership was in the hands of those two women. They did what neither the CEO nor Max had the power to do. They did it well, and they made a difference. How long that difference would last was anybody's guess, but for a period, Spirit was focused and liberated.

For those concerned with impact on the bottom line, the effect might appear minuscule. However, given the fact that prior to the rally there was mounting evidence that a number of important executives were not only exhausted, but also beginning to look for a quick way out, and that after the rally the mood palpably changed, one might argue that the bottom line effect was far from minor.

CHAPTER X

THE FUNCTIONS OF LEADERSHIP:
SUSTAINING SPIRIT WITH STRUCTURE

Gathering and focusing Spirit is the first act of leadership, but left at that point, Spirit will once again dissipate and disperse. Unless it is channeled for the long haul, Spirit raised by Vision and fused in the Collective Story will fly apart. Organizational structure is the pathway of Spirit, and growing appropriate structure is the third function of leadership.

Creating organizational structure is probably what we in the West do best; at least we spend the most time on it. We pay a price for our fixation, however, for all too often structure is seen to be the only thing in an organization. At worst this leads to the denial of Spirit, which cuts us off from the true source of organizational power. Even under the best of circumstances, our obsession with structure causes us to build structure first, and then to try squeezing the Spirit in. The architects understood some time ago that "form follows function" (Sullivan). In short, it is worthwhile considering what you are going to do in a building before you build it. In a similar way structure follows Spirit, and to reverse the order is to invite disaster.

Creating structure before attending to Spirit is like buying a pair of shoes without measuring your feet. It is possible that the shoes will fit, but much more likely that they either will pinch or fall off. Thus, while there are many possible organizational structures, there is no right one in the abstract; only *appropriate ones*, appropriate to the flow of Spirit in that organization.

The current fascination with round, flat, participatory organizations certainly has much to commend it, but it would be a mistake to think that steeply ranked, hierarchical structure is no longer ever appropriate. Hierarchies can, and do, work under the suitable circumstances when the quality of Spirit and the nature of the job at hand fit that particular way of being. For example, when putting out a fire with a bucket brigade, participatory management is not too good an idea. Somebody needs to give the orders, and that is usually the Chief.

Not only is there no one right structure, there may be several useful ones, operational at the same time, as I discovered to my surprise while working with a client. When I first started with them, I asked the CEO for a copy of the organizational chart. He smiled at my question, and just as I was about to say something about knowing that it was probably out of date, he broke in to tell me that they didn't have *an* organizational chart, they actually had something like 20 of them. Their business involved some twenty different major projects, each one having very different needs at different times. They literally reconfigured the organization to fit the needs of each project and those who were going to do that job.

Although this approach might seem to be a recipe for confusion, my client had discovered that organizational charts were really only useful for two groups of people: customers and new employees. The former needed the chart in order to know whom to call with a question, while the latter found it a useful security blanket while figuring out their place. Everybody else pretty well knew what was going on, and felt quite comfortable concentrating on the job. And so for every job there was a chart, available to the customer and the new employees. Since the customer was usually only interested in one job, and the new employee would typically only be working on one job, the fact that there were other organizational charts was neither a matter of knowledge nor concern.

GROWING APPROPRIATE STRUCTURE

We may learn a lot about growing appropriate structure from the experience of those who built many of the new university campuses in the United States. It was often the case that these campuses, designed by landscape architects, were stronger on aesthetic appeal than utility, especially when it came to walkways. The architects, seeking balance and symmetry (or whatever other design criteria they might have in their heads) laid out the walkways on which the students would presumably travel. However, after the campuses opened, it quickly became apparent the elegant designs bore little relationship to the actual flow patterns of the students. The result was the creation of muddy pathways going in just about any direction except the ones the architect had in mind. The erection of fences and walls to channel the errant students usually had little effect, and what started out as a marvelous idea became a mess.

Then one day, a blinding flash of the obvious occurred. Don't put in any pathways until you see which way the folks are going to travel. The initial period in this experiment was certainly a mess, but probably no worse than the alternative, in which the prescribed pathways were ignored while the adjacent lawns were destroyed. But given a little time, the tracks were laid down, and all that remained was to pave them. Structure followed flow.

Following the Footprints of Spirit

Building structure to fit and support Spirit is a laudable undertaking, but it requires the ability to "track Spirit." Using the analogy of the college campus, how do we determine the footprints of Spirit in order to be able to pave the pathway into a serviceable all-weather road? The answer (surprise) lies in the stories we tell.

A small consulting group tells a story about a mad dash to the airport. The offices of the group were located about five miles from the local airport and, as with many consulting groups, the airport was the beginning and the end of almost everything. On one occasion a senior consultant began the mad dash. With minutes to spare, he arrived at the airport only to discover the nearby parking lots full. There was nothing to do but throw caution to the winds, break the sound barrier, to say nothing of the local speed limits, and head for the satellite parking. He quickly found a place which, fortunately, was located near the bus stop. Wonder of wonders a bus was there.

Grabbing his bag, he raced to the bus, proud that he could still make his flight. But the driver had gone on a coffee break. The keys were in the ignition. Not wasting a moment, he settled into the driver's seat and drove to the terminal. Looking neither right nor the left, he parked, and made his flight.

With stories like that, it is not difficult to sense the flow of Spirit in the consulting group, a flow which accomplished much, but had little, if any, toleration for elaborate, bureaucratic procedure. Not surprisingly, such structure that they had was honored mostly in its avoidance, and while they constantly vowed to get themselves organized, the truth of the matter was that they were well organized in a fashion that suited the flow of their Spirit perfectly.

AA - Tax/Audit
& AA Consulting

STRUCTURE, TIME AND SPACE

An organization's structure is the unique time-space configuration for that place. Within very broad limits, however, it is Spirit that defines time and space, and not the reverse. When it appears that Spirit has become a prisoner to time and space, that is typically a matter of choice or ignorance.

Obviously there are limits set by the duration of biological life and planetary existence. Sooner or later each of us will pass away, even as all of us will cease when the sun goes out. We do not have much choice about that, but the limits imposed are fairly broad.

By the same token, there are additional limits imposed by other people's time and space, the structure of other constellations of Spirit. But the acceptance of those limits is always a matter of choice. By default or conscious intention, we choose the time and space our Spirit exists in.

Most of the time, unfortunately, the availability of choice remains beyond awareness, and we feel trapped. Occasionally, this will create amusing situations, particularly when we realize how we have become our own worst enemies.

Creating Time

Several years ago, I was leading a five-day conference which was unusual by virtue of the fact that it had absolutely no formal agenda or timetable, except as the group of one hundred chose to create one. At the beginning, people only knew when we opened, when we closed, and the nature of the overall theme.

The conference itself began with an agenda-setting process in which all participants were encouraged to identify those areas of interest they would like to explore around the given topic. These interest areas were given short titles, posted on the wall, and all parties invited to indicate their selection by signing up on the appropriate card. Time and space (where and when) arrangements were proposed by the initiators and negotiated with the potential participants. In something less than an hour and a half, the group of one hundred was ready for business.

The first day of the conference flowed with almost military precision. Working groups met at the times and places specified, and business got done. That evening, however, we had a small party, and the next morning, the conferees were more than a little slow to line up at the starting gate. In fact, by the time we had all assembled, the official starting time of 9:00 a.m. had long since passed. And then of course, coffee had to be drunk and morning greetings exchanged.

While all of this was taking place, I noticed one of the participants becoming more and more agitated. It seems she had scheduled her group to meet at 11:00, and sensing the domino effect, she pleaded with me to stop all the chatter, and get on with the business. For reasons approaching "malice aforethought" I resisted her suggestion, if only because I felt that the coffee and morning greetings were essential to counteract the effects of the night before. The group finally got together at just about 11:00. As for the agitated participant, concern had given way to anger, with apoplexy near at hand.

When the time seemed right, I asked all the participants to take out their watches and announced that, for those who cared, the time was precisely nine o'clock. The immediate reaction was quizzical, followed by confusion, and eventually round-faced grins. *We had all learned that time is what you make it*. As usual, the Third Immutable Principle will apply. Whenever it starts is the right time.

When Spirit is trapped in a time inappropriate to itself, and the functions to be performed, the results can range from mild discomfiture to total system breakdown.

Different Times

Western travelers to third world countries often find the nature of time there not to their liking. Everything (from the Western point of view) is late, slow, or never happens at all. Until the internal clocks are reset, and one becomes used to the operative story ("mañana") and Spirit, the net result is no small amount of frustration, and occasionally disaster. By the same token, people from other cultures, attempting to operate under the Western sense of time will experience similar difficulty.

Once I attended an international congress on organization development in Mexico. For reasons now obscure to me, the Mexicans had gotten the idea that in order to run a proper conference, it had to be done by the Western rules. Accordingly, they prepared a statement of five "conference norms," which were prominently displayed on the screen at the beginning of the conference, and at the start of each day. Among these was the announcement: "We will start all sessions on time."

It will not surprise any non-Westerner, or anyone who has worked in a non-Western environment, to learn that no session: not the first, the last, nor anyone in the middle ever began "on time." No matter how often the norm was enunciated, everything started when it was ready, and not when the clock pointed to a particular hour.

What was surprising, or at least instructive, was that no matter when events started, everything of importance appeared to have been accomplished. And in fact, more could have been accomplished had time not been spent trying to get everything

to start "on time." The conference had its own internal sense of
rhythm which was highly productive, and had little to do with
the clock. When I mentioned all of this to my hosts, they
smiled enigmatically, but I did notice that as the conference
progressed, the organizers began to treat the announcement
more as a joke than as an expected behavior. In doing this, I
believe they honored the "shape" of the conference spirit with
a time that was appropriate. At the very least, they became
observably more comfortable with "their time" as opposed to
the "right time," for their time was the right time.

Many Times

The truth of the matter is that there are many times,
each one appropriate to the Spirit of a given place, and the
job that needs to get done. With a little thought and effort, it
is quite possible to move from one time to another.

I am told that there is a small town somewhere in the
American Midwest, which for reasons of its own, runs on two
totally different times without problem. This particular town (as
many such places) is laid out around the intersection of two
highways, one running north-south, and the other east-west.
For half of the year, the whole town runs on the same time,
but come Daylight Savings Time, things change because of the
needs of the people and their work.

On the east side of town, a large dairy cooperative
serves the local dairy farming community. On the west side of
town, there is a small manufacturing plant, which distributes its
product all over the country. When Daylight Savings Time
comes in the spring, the west side of town makes the shift

easily. Indeed, those who work in the plant have to shift in order to be aligned with their customers and suppliers, who are also on the new time.

Those on the east side of town, whose lives revolve around the dairy cooperative, have another consideration. While humans can easily switch the hands of a clock, cows operate rather differently. Milking time happens when it is time to milk. Thus the time in the east is milk time, and not clock time. Daylight Savings Time never happens in the east, and the town has two times.

Under most circumstances, having two times is not a difficulty, except at lunch. It seems that the town's only restaurant is located at the highway junction, and for luncheon partners from opposite sides of the town, it is essential to specify not only what time they would meet, but whose time they had in mind. And so there has developed the local convention of "fast time" and "slow time." I can't remember which one is which, but all the locals can, and life moves in an orderly way. Time is appropriate to Spirit.

SPACE AND SPIRIT

Just as time is very often taken as a given, immutable reality, so also space. Spirit then may become a prisoner of space instead of space being the appropriate site for Spirit and its activities.

Almost everyone has had the experience of walking into drab surroundings and feeling his or her spirit sag. When gray walls seem to close in from any point of view, the likelihood of spirited enterprise is remote indeed. But it is a mistake to presume that bigger is better, or that fresh paint will automatically make Spirit soar. While it is true that pleasant surroundings appear to have a positive impact on productivity, the connection is neither automatic nor necessary. The critical issue is always appropriateness.

A case in point was the glistening new office building which became the regional headquarters for Apex Corporation.[14] Apex is and was a dynamic, fast growing, high-tech firm specializing in computer applications for the military. Their original office facilities were notable for just about anything but "glitz." They occupied cramped space over a Chinese laundry, across the street from Harry's Bar.

The history of the company's growth could easily be traced by observing the marks of old walls left indelibly imprinted in the floor. As projects came and went, walls were moved, and space, albeit cramped, was created to meet needs.

[14] Apex is a pseudonym to protect the innocent.

But no matter what was done, there never seemed to be enough space. People were falling all over each other, but surprisingly, that condition was less a problem than a benefit. The close proximity turned out to produce a rich working environment in which productive interchange was almost inescapable.

The walls themselves became icons of history. Pert Charts, cartoons, naughty and irreverent inscriptions bounded the space with colors and shapes unique to Apex's history. The highs and lows of past engagements served as reminders and challenges for the tasks at hand.

When really important work had to be done, requiring the best from everybody, Harry's Bar was more often than not the site of choice. What could not, or would not, get done in the normal working space moved across the street.

Then the decision was made to change the space. As it happened, a local real estate developer had some land on which he was prepared to erect the grandest building ever seen, at least in that part of the world. Seven stories tall, or thereabouts, with a soaring lobby and a glass-enclosed elevator rising in the center. It was nothing, if not grand. But it certainly was not Apex.

Formerly close working colleagues found themselves separated by whole floors, and even on the same floor running shoes were appropriate. Contrasted with the old situation, where everybody knew each other and what they were doing, the new building created an environment in which some people were frank to admit that they had never even been into the furthest reaches. And as far as knowing who worked there, that was beyond any direct knowledge. Harry's Bar, of course, was a thing of the past, and when people went out, they tended to disperse across the countryside in search of good food, regardless of the lack of good fellowship.

The move changed the Spirit at Apex. One might argue, of course, that the march of progress (if such it was) would quickly outweigh whatever discomfiture of Spirit. And long term, it may well be that the glorious new building would not only look more businesslike, but actually foster such behavior. In the interim, however, it was quite clear that Apex had lost a valued connection with its history. New employees would now enter an environment which looked a lot like every other high-tech organization. The special nuances, to say nothing of the mess, that made Apex, Apex were nowhere to be seen.

Creating Positive Space

The creation of appropriate space for Spirit always begins with Spirit. While aesthetic and other generalized design criteria apply, they must always be related to the Spirit of a place and not some abstract thoughts about the "right way to do things." A strong example appeared during the closedown of a 50-year-old plant.

The plant in question was located in southern California, and for more than half a century it produced a familiar line of products for a Fortune 500 corporation. In addition, it was the center of life for three generations. More than a job, the plant, and the associations which developed around it, created a social fabric which gave meaning and community to those who shared in it. From baseball games to skiing trips, life for many began and ended with the plant.

Suddenly, it was no longer. Rising real estate value and taxes, coupled with stringent environmental restraints, and an aging technology, made it certain that the numbers would never come out right. It was nobody's fault particularly, and the decision to close was inevitable.

Unlike many plant closings, this one was done with a degree of humanity and intentionality which set it apart. A full fifteen months before the gates were to close, all employees were told what was going on.

In addition to providing the people with plenty of time to make the necessary adjustments in their lives, the company committed itself to a level of support during the process of transition which some might find unbelievable. Not only were people offered transfers or generous severance packages, they were also provided with the time and guidance necessary to create their own futures. The plant manager intentionally created a learning community which effectively became a University of the Future. Open to everybody, from senior managers down to forklift drivers, the University of the Future provided the standard fare of classes on résumé writing and interviewing skills, *and* went significantly beyond. Seminars were offered on organizations in transformation, transition management, creating small businesses, using your intuitive self, and a number of others which the conventional wisdom might deem at, or beyond, the edge of the frivolous.

The University of the Future, and the Spirit engendered there, required space to happen. Part of the space was supplied by various hotels, where off-site seminars were conducted, but on the home campus, the focal point was The Technical Skills Development Center. This center was located on a corner of the plant property, and was fitted out with offices and classrooms. It therefore seemed to be the only choice. Outplacement and training staffs were quartered there, and it was expected that people needing services would make the short trip across the parking lot to the facility.

That expectation turned out to be ill-founded, or at the very least, the level of business was nothing like what might have been predicted. It was not that the place was uncomfortable, unattractive, or basically unsuited for the purpose. But the trip across the parking lot was more than a short walk. For first timers, it ended up being the very long journey to the end of their careers at the plant.

Even though everybody knew that the plant would close, and that the future lay elsewhere, that knowledge was exquisitely painful and not to be dwelled on. The pain of ending for many was such that a million reasons could always be found why NOT to make the trip. And even when the trip was initiated, it was not uncommon to see it aborted half way there. Walking through the parking lot almost guaranteed meeting friends, with whom it was all too easy to stop and pass the time, while avoiding the sorrow. The center was the "right place" for many good and practical reasons. But it was not appropriate to the Spirit.

Another space offered itself, not so much by design as by happenstance, which is often the way with space fitting to Spirit. In the rush for closedown, a Special Order, involving hand packing a large amount of the plant's product had been pushed further and further back on the agenda of things to do. That continued to be the situation until a young manager saw an opportunity in the problem. She had noticed that with the advent of closedown, and despite the operation of the University of the Future, time was hanging heavy on the hands of many. Worse than that it was silent time. For reasons of embarrassment or fear, a lot of people simply were not talking through their plans and feelings. She reasoned that if she could just get people doing something together, the time would pass faster, and they would also have the occasion to talk. And so the MASH (Make Amazing Stuff Happen) project was born.

The actual arrangement was anything but business as usual. Everybody in the plant, from senior management on down, was invited to wrap product, indeed they were often recruited as they walked in the door in the morning, or on their way out at the end of their day. The only conditions were that folks must come in pairs. Upon arrival, participants were initiated into the MASH Team, and given T-shirts as a sign of their union. Music, usually rock, formed the background, and decorations of all sorts festooned the otherwise drab environment. Prizes were to be awarded to the super wrappers, and the overall champion team would get the tape recorder on which the music had been played. When things started, the Spirit was definitely up, and so it continued for the best part of a month. The product was wrapped in record time, and as predicted, people found the needed time to talk.

The MASH site became a magic place where people continued to gather long after the project had ended. When it came time to put on a job fair for those still looking for their next act, the MASH area was the site of choice. In retrospect it is clear why that area became as powerful as it did. It was in the plant, and not at the end of a long walk. It was familiar turf to everybody, although it had been made special by the decorations, music, and most especially, by virtue of the quality of Spirit that had been encountered there. By almost any standard, the MASH site would have been the last place to locate the center of the University of the Future, but the truth of the matter is that it was, or became, totally appropriate to Spirit.

Creating "The Book" — Space of a Different Sort

The appropriate space for Spirit does not always have to be between four walls. It may also be between two covers. In the case of the plant closing, a book, was designed to provide an opportunity for all to honor their past, consider their present, and shape their future.

When one thinks of writing a book, it is usual to name the theme, determine the structure, and gather the content, with a single person in charge, otherwise known as the author. In this case, only the theme was named, and then everybody in the plant, even those who had left, were invited to contribute whatever they thought to be relevant under the general headings of Our Past, Present, and Future. The structure emerged from the content, and the "author" was a three-person editorial committee, who put it all together in two days.

Getting a large number of people to contribute to a book is no small task, particularly when they are divided by working shifts and the geography of the plant. The added pressures of closedown made it especially difficult. Thus a space of a different sort was required, which might be called electronic space. Utilizing the computer conferencing system of the corporation, which could be accessed through a large number of terminals in the plant, or by phone from basically anywhere in the world, an anywhere/anytime space was created which people could enter at their pleasure. And enter they did. The offerings ranged from wonderful tales of the early days to thoughtful pieces reconsidering the approach to closedown in which the "lessons being learned" were summarized.

While The Book, as it came to be known, would certainly not displace *Megatrends* from the bestseller list, it was probably more important to the people in the plant than that blockbuster could ever be. The Book represented the structured repository of the Spirit they had known during a most critical period of their lives. On the day the plant closed, copies were available for all.

CONCEPTUAL SPACE — THE GEOMETRY OF OUR MINDS

The discussions so far have generally, and intentionally, avoided the more usual topics considered under the heading of organizational structure, such as organization charts, chains of command and the like. The primary reason is practical: it is much easier to illustrate the appropriateness of structure to Spirit with such earthy tales as MASH. But organization charts, in whatever form, are also essential. They represent a different sort of space and time, which we might call "conceptual." The reality of such things exists only in our thoughts, although the pieces of paper on which they are drawn can serve as a useful reminder of what we had in mind. To speak of an organizational chart is to speak of a pure abstraction.

The geometry we hold in our minds, through which we understand the functions of our organizations, is potent indeed. And like more physical indicators of time and space, it as easily can become a prison, as an aid to Spirit. When our mental geometry describes a multilayered structure with checkpoints at every level, we will inevitably perceive "the top" as being a long way off, and the journey there to be difficult and dangerous. Change that geometry into round or spherical, and suddenly all points become a lot more accessible. Transform the organizational geometry one more time, from single-centered to multi-centered, and in an instant, there is no longer a "top," or "center" at all.

The permanence of the organizational geometry lies not in its abstraction, but rather in its concrete application. Placing the CEO at the "top" of the organization chart is very often made concrete by locating the executive suite on the upper floors of the building. At that point, the mental journey up the chart, becomes a very physical one up the elevator or stairs. It may be that the view is better, or the space more comfortable, but even when that is not the case, the mental geometry apparently persists. The executive suite of Owens Corning Fiberglas, for example, occupies the 28th floor of a corporate office building in Toledo, which has a very nasty tendency to sway in high winds to the point of causing seasickness. Given the fact that Toledo is located but a short distance from the Great Lakes, from which the winds blow strongly and often, meeting senior staff displaying various shades of green, is not an unknown experience.

Despite the fact that the geometry of the organization often assumes the permanence of stone, it remains an abstraction, useful when it channels Spirit in productive directions, but stultifying, or destructive, when it does not. Should negative aspects appear, particularly when the structure has been cast in concrete and steel, it is natural, but unnecessary, to treat the result as an "immutable given." Structure is, and remains, an abstraction from Spirit, and therefore is changeable, even as the mind can change. And when the mind changes, even the Corporate Edifice can be altered.

GROWING STRUCTURE — THE ROLE OF LEADERSHIP

If you will consider the stories above concerning the emergence of appropriate structure (time and space) for Spirit, it may appear that structure was most effective in its late arrival. When problems arose, they were associated with pre-existing, or prematurely imposed, structure. Thus in the plant closedown, the Skills Development Center, although possessing the requisite physical characteristics, never really made it as the focal point for the University of the Future. Instead, the scruffy old shipping room became the critical center of Spirit.

One might conclude from the above that structure is not necessary, and that would be totally erroneous. Structure is the essential pathway of Spirit, but to fulfill that function, it must always follow the footprints; it must be appropriate to Spirit. Allowing and encouraging appropriate structure to emerge is a critical function of leadership, and one that cannot be undertaken lightly.

At this point, it is probably clearer what *not* to do. Above all else, do not impose structure arbitrarily. There is no such thing as the "right" structure, no matter what the current fads may suggest. The function of leadership is to *grow* structure, not impose it. The process is an organic, evolutionary one, the work of a gardener, not a mechanic. Growing structure starts with Open Space (and Open Time), precisely the sort of space in which Spirit appears.

> **The function of leadership is to grow structure, not impose it. The process is organic, the work of a gardener, not a mechanic.**

Working in Open Space

Working in Open Space is not without its problems, particularly for those who equate leadership with control. For them it may appear that Open Space is Nothing, and *how can you control anything with nothing?* This was four-star Admiral Harry Train's question as he became the executive director of the Future of Hampton Roads (FHR) Inc. FHR Inc. emerged as the guiding organization from a massive project of Spirit-building undertaken in southeastern Virginia. In that part of the world, there were nine cities and four counties (Newport News, Norfolk, Virginia Beach and so on — the home of 1.2 million people) who had spent the better part of 300 years, either ignoring each other or in hostile combat. Eventually, a small group of private sector leaders came to the conclusion that they were shooting themselves in the foot. While they sat on some of the finest real estate on the East Coast of the United States, little positive growth occurred because all the available energy was devoted to fighting. With some help from the author, they resolved to make a change which involved creating a positive vision for the future, and essentially telling a new tale for the region. How they proceeded is a long story, but succeed they did with some very remarkable results.[15] For example, they managed to move their region from being the 149th market place in the United States into the Top 50 category as number 29.

---

[15] The details of this particular adventure are laid out in my book <u>Spirit</u> as the final case study.

Early in this project, the community leaders created the Future of Hampton Roads as a base of operations, and recruited the Admiral to direct it. As the Admiral and I were sitting outside the board room, waiting for the board to make their selection official, he looked over at me and said, "Harrison, what have you gotten me into?" I am not sure that my answer really helped him, but I said, "Well Admiral, it is rather like being given the whole U.S. Army (which at that point had roughly 1.2 million people), which, for its total history, had been operating as 13 autonomous and hostile units, with the assignment of getting all the troops together without a shred of line authority." "Oh," said the Admiral. To his undying credit, the Admiral succeeded beyond what even he would have admitted was the wildest of dreams. And he did it by learning to operate in Open Space.

Open Space is a far different beast, with very different rules, than the strict hierarchical structure the Admiral had left as Commander of the Atlantic Fleet, in which things *supposedly* got done through "Command and Control." Open Space is an open space precisely because it is bounded. It is bounded by the central Vision which establishes the context within which activity may take place. We are talking about THIS product and THIS market, as opposed to all others. Furthermore, the boundary of Open Space is strengthened and clarified as the Collective Story is woven, giving color and shape to what might take place. So Open Space has a certain shape and location, if you will, but its critical quality is the absence of "a mess of stuff" inside.

Open Space stands as an invitation, a big, attractive, and do-able invitation, for Spirit to enter and grow. There is, however, one fast, and unfailing, method for killing Spirit: to prematurely fill the space with a "mess of stuff." Filling space is almost irresistible. Forget for the moment, whatever needs leadership might be experiencing in terms of getting themselves organized, and appearing to know what they are doing; the press from the outside is almost overwhelming. All those who have been attracted to the Vision, and empowered through the Collective Story, will understandably "want to get the show on the road." And, more often than not, they want somebody to TELL them. The normal form for "telling" is a lengthy list of missions, goals and objectives, set in a rigid time table, with appropriate authority and responsibility established.

There will come a time for TELLING, but if it comes too soon, the Spirit will die. Leadership must honor the space, and avoid telling, until it is the right time. Remember the Third Immutable Principle? There is no magic formula for determining the "right time." It is always a fine judgment call, balanced between premature closure, which will kill Spirit, and unending delay, which will dissipate Spirit. But if there is any rule of thumb, it is something like: Wait as long as you can stand it, then wait just a little bit more. Nature abhors a vacuum, and people want to fill up Open Space with structure, so if error is to be made, err on the side of openness.

If Vision is clear, and the Collective Tale well told, the manifestation of structure will occur at the Right Time with amazing rapidity. Contrary to popular wisdom, which views the structuring of an organization as an unending, difficult task, it is almost pathetically easy when the conditions are right. For example, the 40-odd private sector leaders involved in the Future of Hampton Roads Inc. created an effective organizational structure for FHR Inc. during the course of one day. Twenty-four hours later it was a legal entity with bylaws, bank account, and a board of directors. When the Spirit is up and clear, structure happens. Indeed, if there is any difficulty at all in the articulation of structure, that should be taken as *prima facie* evidence that the time was not right. Structural decisions, like good wine, spoil when taken ahead of their time.

> **Leadership grows appropriate structure by honoring the Open Space, maintaining the boundaries, and encouraging Spirit to find its own form.**

FROM LEADERSHIP TO MANAGEMENT

When the time is right and structure emerges, the mode of operation passes from leadership to management. The importance of management, good management, cannot be over emphasized, but management has its place. Leadership liberates. Management controls. Leadership operates in Open Space, while management operates the system. Leadership invokes and invites Spirit to lay down new footprints. Management paves the path, keeps the troops on schedule, and on the road.

Appropriate structure increases focus, while removing side eddies, distractions and obstacles. It allows for all available energy to be targeted on the task at hand, which is what productivity and profits are all about. Rather than engaging in endless re-inventions of the wheel, good structure and good management insure that the task at hand is accomplished within resources and on schedule, with something left over for the bottom line. Management is essential.

But it is worthwhile remembering that management only works in a given context, and where there is general agreement as to what the context is. Should the context change, or the agreement fail to exist, it is a whole new ball game. Managers control. That is their job. Control, in turn, depends on the ability to measure. As the old saw reminds us, "If you can't measure it, you can't manage it." Measurement, however, always depends on the context, from which it is calibrated. Place a Western manager in a third world context, and he or she will often complain that nothing happens "on time." Right thought, but no agreed context. The problem is not that things do not happen on time, but rather that there is not agreement on what time is.

Leadership and Management — a Necessary Polarity

Listening to current conversations, it seems that we may have gotten ourselves into a totally nonproductive discussion, even argument, about leadership and management. At worst it appears that one or the other is the only thing, and nothing

110

could be further from the truth. In fact leadership and management constitute a polarity, or continuum, which does not allow for *either/or* thinking. *Both/and* is the rule, although there are times when one side will predominate. In stable times, when environments tend to remain constant, and systems are not constantly stressed or destroyed, management will inevitably be the dominant mode of operation. However, when the environment radically alters, and systems are incessantly thrown into the chaos of Open Space, leadership must come to the fore.

We have experienced a number of years characterized by reasonable stability, and for understandable reasons, management has been the dominant mode. The fruits of good management are everywhere apparent in the remarkable advance of productivity and efficiency. But it is safe to say that the times have changed, and that the global context is being reset. At such a time we all experience the Open Space of ending and opportunity. The old structures give way, and time and space must be redefined to fit the new manifestations of Spirit.

All observable signs suggest that now is the time of leadership. And indeed, genuine leadership is required, but it must be leadership *linked* to good management. The rapid passage of events has so foreshortened the life cycles of our organizations that leadership and management must hold together, and conceptually this means abolishing the notion that there are leaders and managers. The fact that some individuals are more comfortable in one mode or the other does not obviate the necessity for each of us to lead and manage — while simultaneously being acutely aware of the context. As the context changes, so must the mode of our operation.

Leadership invokes and invites Spirit to lay down new footprints.
Management paves the path, keeps the troops on schedule, and on the road.

CHAPTER XI

THE FUNCTIONS OF LEADERSHIP:
BEING THERE AT THE END

All good things come to an end. This is true of boxes of candy and outstanding human systems. To restate the Fourth Immutable Principle, "When it is over it is over."

The second law of thermodynamics tells us that all systems tend toward entropy, which is a concise way of letting us know that eventually the energy which drives a system becomes so regularized, and evenly distributed all across the system, that it is no longer clearly in evidence. Strange as it may seem, the First Law of Thermodynamics, which asserts that energy is neither created nor destroyed, is not contravened for, all appearances to the contrary, the energy is still there, it is just homogenized into sameness. There is no "difference that makes a difference."[16]

The same may be said about human systems. It is not that the originating Spirit has disappeared, it is only locked up in the Organizational Structure. What began as a flash of Spirit manifest in Vision, focused through a collective tale, and made real and concrete in structure with its own time and space, eventually becomes boring.

---

[16] Gregory Bateson, <u>Steps to an Ecology of Mind</u> (Ballantine Books, 1972).

> ## The more perfectly an organization runs, the closer it is to its end.

It is paradoxical to the extreme, but the more perfectly an organization runs, the closer it is to its end. As structure is built, and management refines and operates that structure, the level of efficiency and effectiveness, not to mention profitability, goes up. The driving Spirit which energizes an organization is channeled ever more narrowly to the task at hand. Nothing is wasted, nothing is spun off, everything is focused on the bottom line, however that might be defined. The good news is that the machine works well. The bad news is that it is boring.

Owens Corning Fiberglas was a superbly managed organization. It dominated the market it created with the invention of its major product, was profitable to a fault (which made it a tasty takeover target), and it seemed to many that OCF would simply last forever. But when I interviewed a number of executives in those halcyon days before Wicks, I discovered a curious and constant refrain in the stories they told. On the one hand they were quick to acknowledge the positive. Their compensation was adequate, training and development programs constantly available, a well defined and smoothly functioning reward system in place, but —

But? Who could ask for anything more? What possibly could be missing from this picture of general perfection? The answer usually came in words like "But, you know, we haven't had any fun in 10 years."

Somehow, the excitement and adrenaline surges of the "old days" had disappeared. The good news was that the system worked, and worked exceedingly well. The bad news was, it was dull. The pathways for Spirit in that place had been so carefully laid out and maintained (not to mention guarded) that there was no sense of adventure.

Having fun on the job has not, until recently, been understood as an essential working condition, but truth to tell, when the fun and excitement stop, and boredom sets in, a number of other definitely less desirable effects are almost certainly in the wings. Boredom inevitably produces sloppiness and trouble-makers, a fact well known to parents and nursery school teachers.

Bored employees tend to overlook the details, which translates directly into a decline of quality, and an increase in customer dissatisfaction. Boredom also gives birth to trouble-makers, for the Spirit is still there, it is just feeling claustrophobic. Trouble, of course, can come in many packages. At best it will emerge as harmless pranks, done just to make the time go faster. At worst, trouble comes in packages labeled office bickering, back-biting, nasty rumors, and worse.

Boredom also manifests itself in a decline in creativity. I do not know it to be a fact, but the story at OCF was that they hadn't had a truly new product in 10 years, and that during a time when they maintained an enormous research facility on a 200-acre campus with 1,200 employees.

OCF, to its credit, was by no means blind to these disturbing symptoms. Their response, very much in line with general corporate practice, was an attempt to fix the system. The fix went in two directions. On the one hand there was a heavy investment in quality control: checkers to check the checkers, guided by a super checker. On the other hand, programs were introduced to raise creativity, most particularly an outstanding import from Sweden created by The Foresight Group, and known as *The School for Intrepreneurs*. The school represented an honest attempt to juice up the old system with a good shot of entrepreneurial zeal.

The Wick's takeover intervened before all these "fixes" could be fully played out, but had Wicks not come on the scene, I strongly suspect that the experience at OCF would have paralleled that of all other organizations I know under similar circumstances. The proposed system fixes would not have worked; indeed, they would have been counterproductive. The problem was not that the system wasn't working, but precisely the opposite. The system was doing exactly what it was designed to do, channel Spirit. In doing its job, it was also reaching its intended goals, which were efficiency, effectiveness and profitability. There were, unfortunately, some toxic by-products.

Under the circumstances, the proposed "fixes" really would not have done much good. The increase in quality control only would have further tightened the system, and increased the constraints upon available Spirit. In practical terms the results would appear as reduced flexibility and increased costs. Not exactly what was needed.

As for the School for Intrepreneurs, the intent was laudable, but the outcome could have been disastrous, for as the program released entrepreneurial zeal, even as the system moved toward greater control, something would have had to give. It is possible that the rising young Intrepreneurs really would have made a difference, in which case, the system would have been radically altered. More likely, the system would triumph, and it would be back to business as usual. Neither effort could alter the fact that when it is over, it is over.

The advent of Wicks, with its hostile takeover attempt, short-circuited the process, and may well have saved Owens Corning, but certainly not the OCF that used to be. In the days and months following the tender offer, there was a great deal of conversation about the New Owens Corning Fiberglas. Admittedly there was not a high level of agreement about what the New OCF would be, but I think it was apparent to all that the Old OCF had gone.

Also apparent was an outbreak of Spirit. Although the time immediately surrounding the takeover attempt was painful indeed, resulting in enormous disruption in the lives of many, it surely was not boring. Candid conversations often yielded statements like, "It surely has been rough, but truth to tell, I haven't had so much fun in years. Talk about challenge and performance! It was exciting to know that our corporate life was on the line, which meant that we all had to make a difference."

Even those who left seemed to share some of the excitement, as I found out indirectly from a telephone call by the son of a former executive left on my answering machine. This young man told me that his father was a terminated OCF executive. After 30 years with the company, the shock of termination was no small thing, but when the anger and pain cleared, his father discovered a remarkable thing. He had been imprisoned by a system which had taken all his time, energy and talent. When it all broke down, he climbed on a plane to visit his son. They talked seriously for the first time in 20 years.

WHY WAIT FOR WICKS?

If it is true that there is a certain naturalness of ending, and that inevitably there will come a time when a system has not only fulfilled, but also exhausted its potential, why is it that we sit around until the inevitable is obvious? Why indeed?

There are probably a million ways to candy-coat the answer, but none of them will avoid the final conclusion. We wait because of death. We don't like it. The extremity of this statement is not meant for shock value, but rather to quickly bring the discussion down to where it needs to be. Using the word *death* may appear an overstatement, but I seriously believe that is what we experience when our systems reach their end. In a plant closing or a major downsizing, one has only to visit briefly with those walking out the door, as well as those who remain, to understand the depth of the situation. If it is not death, it is surely the next thing to it. Good "company folks," who spent all of their working lives going to the same place, doing the same thing, hoping the common hope and expecting the common reward, are through.

For better or worse, we define ourselves by what we do. Small children understand this immediately when, with pride or confusion, they say, "My Daddy or Mommy does..." At a cocktail party or in a bar, the answer to the question "Who are you?" is

118

as likely to be your title or profession, as your name. And when that definition no longer applies, life as we knew it, isn't any more.

Of course there are those for whom a job is just a job, and they will walk out of the door with no further thought. But such people are not, nor will they ever become, the heart and soul of an organization. They just fill a slot, anchor a desk, and pass the time. We say of them that their heart is not in it, which means that there is no danger of loosing heart when it is all over. Doubtless there is a place for such people, but should they assume a majority position, the organization is in deep trouble. Without heart there is no commitment, loyalty, and all the other good things that make an organization fly. But with heart, commitment, and loyalty comes attachment. When attachment breaks, pain results. You may not want to call it death, and if so choose another word, but experience has taught me that *the human reaction is the same, no matter what the name.* When it is over, it is over, and that hurts.

Speaking of system-ending as *dying,* not only fits the circumstances, but also brings us to a point where we can honestly talk about the factors involved in our inability to face the situation early on, and proactively. This issue is not knowledge, for we have all known since childhood that what goes up must come down, what begins will end, and that sometime, we will all cease. However, having the knowledge and being able to deal with it, are two separate things. Indeed, we in the West expend extraordinary effort distancing ourselves as far as possible from the reality of death. Until fairly recently, even talking about dying was considered poor form. The cosmetic industry makes a fortune helping us all pretend that those early indicators of approaching demise are not there. And the funeral business seems to be in business to mask the reality of dying so that the corpse looks more alive than the living. Our language continues the charade, for few, if any, ever die. They pass on, fall asleep, go to the other side, take the trip. Nobody dies.

Corporate executives are no less averse to the downside. Everything must be "beginning and new" with no thought of ending or passing from the scene. Annual reports are replete with success stories and new ventures, but the ones that have ended warrant only a footnote, if mentioned at all. Consultants and trainers are equally guilty, offering six magic bullets for the attainment of power (read excellence), but nary a word about what to do when it all falls apart. Shortsighted this may be, but quite understandable, for who would pay to be told that all good things come to an end? It is surely better to remain in ignorance, even pretended ignorance.

In this case, ignorance is not bliss, and certainly not when the inevitable becomes reality. But it is no wonder that the end of a system, organization, or corporation, always seems to come as a surprise, with absolutely no advance preparation.

LEADERSHIP AND DYING:
MAKING A GOOD ENDING

The Japanese have a curious concept which they call "a good death." To Western ears this is complete, oxymoronic contradiction. How could death possibly be good? Leaving aside the details for the moment, the mere existence of the phrase points out that there are some different ways of looking at death and ending. Both of these realities may be viewed as the total cessation of everything, in which case our typical way of dealing with them makes a great deal of sense. If you can't do anything about something, and it doesn't make any difference anyhow, best to put it as far out of your mind as possible, and get on with the business of the moment.

On the other hand, should it turn out that ending is simultaneously the fulfillment *and* fracturing of finite forms (in our case human systems, be they corporations or something else), then avoiding the end is to avoid the meaning and purpose for which something was created. In a word, evading death usually results in avoiding life. On the other hand, individuals and organizations who drink it all down to the dregs are precisely the ones who live life in full measure.

> **Evading death
> usually results in
> avoiding life.**

121

There is yet another thought hidden in the idea of "a good death." Endings are the necessary precursors to new beginnings. One simply cannot get on with whatever it is that is coming next until, and unless, the present passes. This thought suggests that in avoiding the fact of ending and death, one not only misses out on the fulfillment of present reality, but also the opening of the next act.

These "hidden thoughts" suggest some added dimensions to leadership. We have previously seen the critical role that leadership plays in creating and maintaining the Open Space in which Spirit appears, first in Vision, then in Collective Storytelling, and most recently, when Structure is grown. We now face the ultimate Open Space, when everything falls away. Leadership must be there at the end.

LEADERSHIP AT THE TIME OF ENDING

When a human system, particularly a business, or part of a business, shows the unmistakable signs of ending, the sequence of behavior at the top is, unfortunately, fairly predictable: (1) Ignore it, perhaps it will go away; (2) Deny it, perhaps it isn't so; (3) Find somebody else to blame, so at least you do not get tagged with the failure; and (4) Bail out as quickly as possible with the largest parachute available.

Given the current infatuation with success, coupled with an inability to deal with death (our own or others), this behavior not only makes sense, it is the only behavior possible. But the cost is enormous. In individual human terms such behavior means that at precisely the moment when Spirit needs to be supported and cared for, those who should assume that responsibility disappear. The pain of ending is real, and the despair engendered inescapable, but if that pain and despair are not to last forever, someone, a·leader, must stand in the middle, just to be there and listen. Not a pleasant task, but I think it comes with the territory.

There are additional organizational costs chargeable to the present behavior of many who call themselves leaders. If the time of ending is also the time of fulfillment, what better learning opportunity could possibly present itself to reflect on all that had been done as a basis for doing it better, or differently? When all the business ceases, there is time to see with a clarity unavailable previously. Closing ones eyes, and/or bailing out at a time of learning, is exceedingly wasteful. Obviously this is not a task for the weak-hearted, but nobody ever said leadership was a going to be easy.

ENDINGS AND NEW BEGINNINGS

There was a day, of course, when it seemed that our organizations would go on forever. Incremental changes might come and go, but the expectation was, "Our Corporation Forever." Of course, there were always those moments when really big changes came along, but those moments seemed few and far between, and they could largely be handled by that convenient mechanism I call the Generational Flush. Once every 20 years or so, all the old guys retired, died, or were

123

otherwise pushed aside. At that time, new blood could come in, along with new ideas and approaches. This was known as progress by funerals, and in the interim, there was not much else to do but wait your turn.

We no longer have the luxury to wait for the Generational Flush. Whole businesses, indeed even industries, come and go within a very few years. Maintaining the competitive edge, to say nothing of simple existence, requires that we do in a decade what many before us never had to negotiate in a lifetime. And we can only believe that the pace we experience will increase. If it is not true that all endings create the Open Space within which new beginnings can occur, we better make it so, or throw in the towel right now.

Converting endings to new beginnings obviously requires more than wishing it were so. For when the end comes, Spirit sags, slips away, and sometimes, just plain goes over the hill. New beginnings require new Spirit, or at least getting the old Spirit back together again. Which poses the interesting question: How do you raise Spirit?

CHAPTER XII

THE FUNCTIONS OF LEADERSHIP: RAISING SPIRIT

Raising Spirit is the final task of leadership. It is final in the sense that it is the last one on our list, and also because it represents the critical difference between the continuation of an organization and its ultimate demise.

When an organization simultaneously reaches its fulfillment and its end, the old forms, structures, building, plants and facilities may persist for a period, indeed even hundreds of years, but they are rather like the remains of former civilizations. Empty shells in which life was lived. There may be a few caretakers, hangers on, remnants of former days, but the Spirit of the place moves out pretty quickly.

Separated by several millennia, we may look at the ruins of ancient Greece or Egypt with a certain equanimity, even nostalgic attachment. But when the ruins happen to be your organization or business, such dispassionate contemplation is not likely. Leaving aside all elemental questions about the necessity to earn a living, certain inevitable thoughts will appear about all that might have been done, or could still be done, if the Spirit were available. Question: How do you revive

Spirit, not in the same old form, but in new forms, and new structures, appropriate to the changing environment?

The work of Ilya Prigogene, referred to earlier, offers some suggestions and even hope. As you will remember, Prigogene tells us that systems, when stressed by a changing environment, will move further and further out of equilibrium, seeking to readjust their present form to the new circumstances. Their activity will appear chaotic and random, and as the stress levels increase, so too the crazy efforts at adjustment. Finally, when no further adjustment is possible, the system will either fly apart, or literally "pop," in a radical, discontinuous jump to new, and more appropriate, ways of being in that environment.

If the first part of Prigogene's description sounds rather like a human system at the end of its rope, or more concretely, your business when the competitors have just dropped a real bomb, the stock market crashed, or the Russians declared Peace, it may also be true that there is a "pop" in your future. And "pop" beats "flop" every time. But the question remains. How do you engineer such a thing?

Were it necessary to create an effective approach *de novo*, I suspect that it might be a long time in coming. But the truth of the matter is that the mechanism already exists, and that we, as a species, have worked with, and through it, from our beginning. In contemporary literature, that mechanism is called *Griefwork*, but other ages and traditions would give it a different name. It is the period of mourning, the wake, the requiem, or sitting shiva.

Griefwork is what we, as human beings, do when confronted by death, our own or the death of another.

Virtually all modern research in this area has related to the individual response, but in my experience, precisely the same patterns take place when a whole organization is in jeopardy.[17] What we now know of the process not only enables us to understand and predict with some accuracy the course of events under very trying and tumultuous circumstances, but also to identify, and facilitate, critical points along the way. Whatever else leadership may be about, surely it finds its center of meaning when the chips are down, quite literally, and it is time to raise Spirit.

Before moving on with the "hows" and "whys," I must once again make it exquisitely clear that in using the word "leadership" I do not refer to the leader, titular or otherwise, who, in his or her own power, is expected to pull all of this off. Altruistic and democratic principles aside, there is absolutely no possibility that any one person could accomplish what needs to get done. To recall the New Rules, *The leader is whoever has the ball*, and corollary to that, *Ball hogs die*. I believe these New Rules always apply, but particularly so in those moments when the Spirit is dragging and must be raised up. The complexity of events, coupled with the strain and stress of the situation, requires that each be leader to the other. We all make it together, or nobody makes it at all.

---

[17] The seminal work in this area was done by Elizabeth Kübler-Ross as reported in her book On Death and Dying (Collier Books, 1970).

GRIEF AT WORK

The experience of grief is known to us all in those moments when a loved one dies, a relationship ends, or a lifework is over. That lifework may be your individual life, or a life defined in, and through, a particular organization, but the feeling of loss and the act of grieving will take place.

What most of us take as an intense feeling, which affects us, is also a constructive process through which we honor the past, acknowledge the present, and set off for the future. It is our way of gathering our Spirit and moving to a new form. The power of the process is such that, in its midst it is difficult, perhaps impossible, to know anything other than: it began, continues with pain, and eventually ends. But, in fact, there are definite stages along the way, and while that knowledge may do little to ease the immediate pain, recognizing the stages in their passage can do much to orient you, and help you help others.

THE STAGES OF GRIEF AT WORK

- Shock/Anger
- Denial/If Only
- Memories
- Open Space
- Imagination
- Vision

128

Griefwork begins with the moment of ending or its imminent approach. Its first manifestation is *Shock and Anger*. The response is purely physiological, and is nothing more than breathing in and breathing out, strongly, as in "ooooooh damnnnnn! The good news is that the patient is still breathing, and in moments of shock, cessation of that life-giving function is a real possibility. But as a long-term strategy, it does little more than keep life going, and the Spirit alive, until something else can be done.

First aid is administered by the next step, which I call *Denial/If Onlies*. Denial is the pretense that nothing has happened, that life will surely go on as it always has. In an organizational setting, denial is expressed in words like, "They can't close this plant down. How are they going to serve the whole region from those idiots on the other coast?"

When that kind of masking no longer works, the *If Onlies* start, as in, "If only we had done something sooner — listened to that consultant/not listened to that consultant." The reality is, it is all over, but Denial and the If Onlies serve to push the pain off to some safer distance. In themselves they do absolutely no good in terms of materially altering the situation, but what they do do is critical. They provide distancing and surcease from the intense pain of ending. Just what a bandage, or anesthesia, does for a wound.

As the irreversible reality of the situation sinks in, albeit somewhat numbed by the anesthesia of denial, the healing process begins in earnest, but here, as in many points in life, it is necessary to go backward in order to make progress. The mechanism is *Memory*. In the vacuum of ending, the memories flow through, with thoughts of all the things that were, and are no longer, might have been, and can never be. The sweet ones, the sad ones, the mad ones, the bad ones ... all pass in review. For those watching this stage, it may well seem like a useless, and interminable, retreat to the past. Verbally it will sound much the same as the previous stage of denial. But there is an important difference. Whereas denial was living in make-believe, the passage of memories is a serious acknowledgement of the past, with the clear recognition that it is gone. Far from being useless, it is essential to honor and release the past before the future ever becomes a possibility. The Story, which bounds Spirit, is being rewritten and prepared for a new tale that will be told.

After a while memories slow and eventually cease. There is nothing more to say. All the heroes have been identified, and the major events reviewed. What remains is silence and pure *Open Space*.

Open Space is initially experienced as being profoundly *down in the dumps*, bereft of anything. Call it despair, for it is the empty agony of ending. There is nothing left, nothing to do, and no hope of bringing it all back again. Neither anger, denial or memory can restore what is no longer. It is over.

If the pain is intense, there is also a sweetness in that pain, reminiscent of the first snow in early winter. The summer is past. The leaves lie dead on the ground. In the silence, the first flakes fall. There is profundity and awesomeness in that moment of silence, a holy moment, a moment filled with wholeness[18] and completion. In the absence of all the things that should be done, could be done, or might be done, one

---

[18] Whole, health, and holy all share a common root, the Old English *hal*.

finally can confront the searing questions: Why do anything at all? What is really important? What is worthwhile doing? What does it all mean anyhow?

"Nothing," may be the answer returned. And if so, there is little to do but acknowledge the obvious, as Spirit goes on its way. Difficult to do, but it is essential to honor that answer, no matter what other plans might be affected. Even if it were possible to plead and cajole, appealing to corporate loyalty, family pride, or whatever else may have persuasive power, a verbal turnaround would do little good. When one has looked into the depths and seen no future, there is no meaningful leverage. Nothing times nothing is, unfortunately, nothing. With nothing to give and nothing to gain, nothing will be accomplished.

But there is another possible outcome should despair turn to *Imagination*. In the silence of ending, when there is nothing left to be done, the ground is cleared of all the "shoulds," "oughts," and "musts." Now it is possible to think of the "might bes," and the "what ifs." No longer constrained by what was, everything now becomes possible. Pure possibility is the seed bed of *Imagination*.

Imagination cannot be forced, but it may be invited, even as Spirit will not be coerced, but may be invoked. The proper invitation to Imagination is not to issue the next five-year plan, or provide the full-blown description of coming attractions. The invitation is always a question. The form may be various, but the substance will always be something like, *What are you going to do for the rest of your life?*

Questions maintain the Open Space within which Imagination and Spirit can grow. The power of the questions lies in their capacity to evoke, creating a sense of futurity, the mere possibility that end is not all, and that beginning is at hand. An invitation extended is no guarantee of acceptance, but if Spirit enters, and Imagination is sparked, it will become manifest in statements like, "You know, the old organization was really grand, but we never could quite reach the potential I'd hoped for. I wonder if ..." Imagination plus wonder creates Vision, from which futures are made.

IMAGINATION PLUS WONDER CREATES VISION, FROM WHICH FUTURES ARE MADE

Thus we have completed the cycle, returning to the moment from which we began, when Spirit is evoked by Vision. But if the journey has been an effective one, Spirit renewed is not the same old thing with fresh paint. As the old Vision, Collective Story, and Structure of time and space, fall away, victim to a changing world, new manifestations of Spirit emerge. Related for sure, but now appropriate to a changed world. The process of Transformation moves on.

LEADERSHIP AND THE PROCESS OF GRIEF

Whatever else leadership may be able to accomplish, it cannot *do* griefwork for anybody. That, fortunately or unfortunately, is something that individuals must do for themselves, even if they all do it together. Nor can leadership minimize the pain, or somehow protect those who grieve from their grief. Humanitarian concerns may strongly suggest the opposite, and when those concerns are blended with holdovers from the present dominant view of leadership, the temptation to intervene may become almost irresistible. But resisted it must be, first because it is useless, but most important, the mere attempt at intervention may retard or abort the process, a process through which individuals and organizations evolve and transform. No pain, no gain.

The reference to *holdovers from the present view of leadership* probably needs elaboration. As long as leadership is viewed as the exclusive prerogative of the one, or the few, to be exercised for the benefit (or detriment) of the many, the basic mode of relationship between leaders and followers will be some form of passive dependency. At worst this means treating followers as "those idiots," although advanced leaders in the old mode seem to be moving towards an enlightened paternalism—maternalism.

The master—servant relationship may work well in more ordered times, and for sure it does wonderful (albeit superficial) things for the egos of leaders and the security needs of followers, but when the times become chaotic, the relationship not only is unworkable, it is counter-productive. At precisely the moment when all of us must take maximal responsibility for ourselves, that responsibility is denied. No one can negotiate the path of Transformation for another.

Obviously there are cases of real need and genuine incapacity (mental, physical and social), but when incapacity is presumed, that presumption often becomes a self-limiting, and self-fulfilling prophesy. So the issue is not a matter of absolute "Do's and Don'ts," but rather of presumptions. Presume incapacity, and it will likely be found, or created. Presume capacity for responsible action, and you may well be surprised. In no event, however, can our presumptions change the reality. Negotiating the process of Transformation is something that can never be done for another. Transformation, like death (because it involves death) is a solo activity. In the words of the old spiritual, "You got to walk that lonesome valley by yourself." [19]

[19] To say that transformation is a solo process might suggest that "organization transformation" is a non-reality. Indeed there are many who would argue that case, and tell us to forget organization, and deal only with individuals. The issue, in my view, is not individual versus organization, but rather that neither fundamentally exist. What is is Spirit, which comes to form as individuals, or (collectively) as organizations. The situation is not unlike that confronted by physicists relative to energy. For them, energy is, although one may choose to talk about it as either waves or particles. To ask which one is right is to invite the answer, "whichever one is useful." We would all agree that no organization has ever existed without individuals, but I would suggest that the reverse is also true. We become who and what we are only in the context of our organizations, be they family, company, or country. A further discussion of this point will be found in my book Spirit.

LOVE IS WHAT LEADERSHIP *CAN DO*

Leadership in the Process of Grief, or more broadly in the course of Transformation, is critical, but it does not play out according to the old rules. *The prime function of leadership is to Love*, and to manifest that love by (1) really being there at the end, (2) maintaining the Open Space, and (3) evoking The Question.

The Two Faces of Love

The word, *love* is used in so many ways as to have almost lost its meaning, referring to everything from raw fornication to some idealized state, and even the Divine Being (as in "God is Love"). Perhaps the normative use is *acceptance*.

I am clear that Love includes acceptance, but I believe there is more. Love in my experience always has two faces, a face of acceptance AND a face of challenge. It is never either/or, always both/and, and the power of love is manifest in the Open Space created by the two.

Love as Acceptance

The first face of love is unconditional acceptance — taking others just the way they are, where they are, and how they are — with no questions asked. It is non-judgmental to a fault. The good news of acceptance is that when we find ourselves accepted, we can more easily accept ourselves as we are. No justification. No rationalization. No apologies.

But acceptance has its down side. Without standards, life turns to mush. Without rigor, thinking becomes sloppy. Without judgment, anything goes. Pure acceptance leaves you just where you are, and never urges you to become everything you could be.

Love as Challenge

The other face of love is radical challenge, a challenge potentially so extreme that you are catapulted into new ways of being. The standards are set, the expectations are there, the judgment is real. Mushy life won't do. Sloppy thinking is unacceptable. Challenge is the road to fulfillment. But challenge by itself is disastrous, for it creates a life of unmitigated harshness.

The Open Space of Love

Neither face of love will work alone. While we may prefer the comfort of acceptance, and it certainly is comfortable, we require the stringent slap in the face of challenge. But it must always be challenge grounded in acceptance, and acceptance excited by challenge. In personal terms, we may address each other as follows: "I take you just the way you are, and expect you to become everything of which you are capable — and more."

Love is neither acceptance or challenge, it is rather the Open Space created by the tension of the two. Maintaining that tension (dialectic, polarity, call it what you will) is no easy task. It is always tempting to give in to the comfortableness of

136

acceptance, or to lose patience, and issue an ultimate challenge. But the depth of our love is measured by the breadth of the Open Space. *Partial Love* is one or the other. *Little Love* is marginal acceptance and minimal challenge. *Great Love* is acceptance and challenge without boundary.

Although this notion of Love may appear different, and perhaps strange, it is not without precedent. In Indian mythology, the two faces of Shiva (destroyer and creator) create the same polarity. From the Tao comes the Yin and the Yang to the same effect. And in the Torah (Old Testament to the Christians) there is Yahweh's (God's) *mishpat* (Judgement) and *chesed* (loving kindness) appearing in and through His essence, which is Love (*Ahabh*). Those traditions, at least, understand mankind to reach fulfillment in the presence of the love of god(s), and that Love is always manifest in the polarity of acceptance and challenge.

LEADERSHIP, LOVE AND GRIEF

When the end comes, and Grief commences, loving leadership is essential, and that love will manifest itself in some very concrete ways, by really being there, maintaining the Open Space, and evoking The Question.

Being There in Love

The first, and possibly the most difficult manifestation of Love, is to be there, right in the middle of all of the grief and chaos. Not just as a visible body, although that may be the only possibility sometimes, and certainly physical presence is usually better than none at all. But being there means really being THERE, accepting the folks and the reality of ending just the way it is, while simultaneously expecting and urging the new reality into being.

In more specific terms, this means being open and available to everything, the pain, the tears, the loneliness, the feelings of self-doubt, the intimations of meaninglessness. As a leader you can't change any of that, nor can you ultimately (or proximately), shield your fellows from the searing effect. Your presence is made more difficult, not to mention painful, by the same feelings in yourself. But leadership at a distance is not possible. As Harry Truman is reported to have said, "If you can't stand the heat in the kitchen, get out."

None but a fool would underplay the cost of such proximity. When the tears of others become your tears, when their fear is your own, the effect is not pleasant. It might be made more bearable were you able to maintain an Olympian distance, but more often than not, that escape route is denied for the simple reason that the tears of others are, in fact, your own, even as the fear is held in common. Unless you just dropped in from some other planet, you are all going through it together.

If the cost is steep, the reward is higher. As the Process of Grief works its way through from Anger to Denial, past

Memories, down into the dumps, and on to Imagination, and then Vision, dissolution turns to triumph, chaos to order.

All of which brings up an interesting question: How do you stand it? For those who persist in playing by the old rules, the answer is stark. You can't. If there is any lingering thought that the leader can, and must, always be in control, taking everything onto him or herself, truly Being There is not possible. Sooner or later that sort of leader will find it necessary to take a quick trip to the executive suite, never to be seen again. Or if seen, then always through some safe protective shield, the Official Appearance, as it were.

Sticking it out "in the kitchen" is never something that can be done alone. The idea that we all must be leaders to each other is not a matter of democratic ideal, but practical necessity. Under the extreme conditions of Transformation, in the middle of the Process of Grief, it is inescapably true that the leader is *Whoever has the ball*, and for sure, *Ball hogs die.*

Maintaining Open Space

The task of leadership, at the onset of the Process of Grief, is to do nothing, or certainly as little as possible. No schedules can be set, lectures given, MBO's prepared. However, if no *thing* can be done, much must be accomplished under the heading of creating space: establishing the time, place, and permission to get on with the business.

The initial stages of grieving simply have to roll out, and leadership must see that the opportunity for all that to occur is available. Above everything else, it is imperative to recognize that there is no possibility of arbitrarily shortening the process or skipping stages. Shock and Anger are there, and must be expressed and accepted. Allowing for a collective "ooooooh-damnnnn," or the equivalent, is essential. No attempts to muffle the noise, make things seem polite and proper, or downplay the intensity of feeling with soothing words of consolation, will have any useful effect. Indeed they will be completely non-productive. Shock not followed by anger usually means that breathing has stopped. And anger, unexpressed, inevitably goes underground to eat out stomachs and poison future working relationships.

The same is true with Denial. Although cooler and more rational heads will see that the pretense of continued denial is only pretend, the anesthetic quality of denial is critical to the moment. No exhortations to "Deal with reality," will change the fact that, at the moment, reality is too painful to be dealt with. Some people never will deal with the reality of ending, and they will be lost to the possibility of new beginning, but even they must be given the space to make that choice. Nobody can do it for them, nor can it be done before they are ready. When it is time, it is time — and not before.

When grief moves us to deal with the Memories, the role of leadership can become more overt by creating special times and places, even formalized ones, where the memories can be honored. This is the function of the Irish wake, but you don't have to be Irish to gather the benefit. A special time to honor the heroes, and salute the mighty deeds, all in the context of a dinner and a glass or two, won't hurt. But no matter what, DO NOT STOP THE PROCESS. Heros unsung, and deeds not honored, will surely lie restless in the grave, and never become available to inspire the evolving future.

Honoring Heroes is best done with love. It is essential that they, and their deeds, be taken at face value, just the way they were. For only in doing that can we really appreciate, for better or worse, what has transpired. But dealing with Heroes only at the level of acceptance is not sufficient, for then we never ask what could have been done. What are the possible implications of their contributions? The function of Memories, as Grief works, is not only to let go of the past, but also to lay the ground work for whatever comes next. It is the front edge of a learning process which can take us from where we were toward whatever we might become. And the driving engine of that is critical judgment. Love maintains the Open Space in which Heroes can be seen for what they were, and learned from, as a guide to possible futures.

A truly profound moment for leadership appears in the depths, when the memories have passed, and the silence of ending is deafening. The temptation to break that silence will prove almost irresistible, but if yielded to, the moment will be lost. For concealed in that moment are the seeds of the future which must be allowed to germinate. In the clarity of ending, when everything else is gone, comes the extraordinary opportunity to consider what it all means. Don't waste it. Honor the Open Space with the dignity of silence. In that silence wonder may appear.

Ask The Question

There will come a time when wonder turns to imagination, but leadership cannot rush to fill in the details. The critical point is the question: What are you going to do with the rest of your life? The posing of that question will mark the shift from ending to new beginning, and it is the unique task of leadership to sense the moment when the question is ripe. No magic formula applies here, and clock-time is entirely useless, for that question will set its own time: indeed, time will start anew with the posing of the question.

It would be a consummate error to suppose that at this point leadership by the Old Rules may now reemerge, with the leader lining up the troops to await their answer. The question will be asked by all of us, to each of us, in a thousand different ways. It may be quite direct, or more often than not, the critical question will be posed in the beckoning rays of a dawning sun, suggesting that a new day might just come. Or in the hungry cry of a newborn child reminding us that life begins anew. Each of us has different ears and different eyes, but all of us may become leaders to each other by offering the question in ways that may be seen and heard.

Asking the question in Love is the deepest act of leadership. For just as the question creates the space within which the quest for new life may be pursued, it is Love that releases the Spirit for the journey. Love-as-Acceptance creates the conditions in which things may be taken just the way they are, allowing the realization that it really is over. We really can let go and move on. Love-as-Challenge points the way, not with

142

a detailed plan that must be followed, but rather the expectation of future fulfillment.

DO WE REALLY HAVE TO GO THROUGH ALL THIS?

Doubtless there are times when we might wish that the ruler of the universe had consulted us prior to setting up the original design, for surely we could have figured out a better way. But in fact, I strongly suspect that the Great Cosmic Being (by whatever name) has already given us precisely what we are asking for. For better or for worse we have been left with the responsibility for deciding and designing what we are to become. But nobody ever suggested responsibility comes for free, and quite obviously some people, sometimes, handle it better than others.

Being stuck with the process doesn't mean, however, that we can't learn to do it better. And in fact, I think the story of the moment is that we are being given endless opportunities to do just that. It may have appeared in our discussions above, that the process of transformation and the work of grief only take place in the megabuster situations, when markets collapse, industries end, and business go out of business. While it is certainly easier to see the process in such extreme situations, I think the reality is that the precipitating events of Transformation are occurring ever closer together. No longer are they separated by millennia, or even the comfortable twenty year cycle marked by the Generational Flush. Transformation is ongoing, and transformations lap and pile on top of each other. We are quickly moving from the old slide presentation into the great motion picture show.

In practical detail, this means that what was once a twenty year, or longer phenomenon, which we could afford to wait for, and then hope to muddle through, is now an everyday occurrence. Unless we wish to be constantly surprised, we have the opportunity to handle it better. The opportunity is made richer by the fact that not only are major transformations coming with greater frequency, but there are a whole bunch of them going on all around us simultaneously, many of which we are hardly aware.

What may be a "precipitating event" for you is a matter of minor concern to me, and *vice versa*. So, for example, as president of a company it may make little existential difference to you that the product line for which I have given blood, sweat, and tears, is about to be terminated. You see it as progress. For me it is a disaster.

Sitting where I sit, it is the end of the world, or at least my world, which after all is the only one that counts for me. It is quite possible, indeed highly probable, that I will have a number of unkind things to say about you. That is called Shock and Anger. But I also have the opportunity to seize the particular moment as an occasion for evolution. Even more than that, I could also learn a great deal about the process, so the next time things fall apart, as surely they will, I will be ready.

The bottom line is quite simple. There was a day when the call for leadership came once a millennia, century or decade. Leaders emerged to answer the call, and we judged them to be unique, awesome individuals. At the moment, the call is going out constantly, so we all have the opportunity, and necessity, to try. Fortunately, I think the secret is out. The solitary leader is gone. We are all leaders.

CHAPTER XIII

THE SPIRIT OF LEADERSHIP
(THE LEADER'S SPIRIT)

I have an Indian friend and colleague, who is the vice president for human resources of a large hotel group. Like many of his peers, my friend grew up in a Hindu family, and until the age of 12 or 13, went through what we might now call the consciousness-raising program common to the Hindus. He also participated in Western style education through preparatory school and university. When he had completed his course of study, he, along with many others of his generation in India, found the old ways somehow not in tune with the business environment of the late 20th century. Quantitative methods, behavioral science and a variety of other approaches, had much more to do with the bottom line.

Then, for reasons which have never been shared with me, he made a remarkable discovery. As effective as his business school methods were in terms of manipulating and interpreting the bottom line, the bottom line became positive and meaningful only in a context of inspired human performance. When the Spirit was up, good things happened, and when it was not, no amount of number crunching was going to change the result. My friend realized what has been suggested here. Spirit is important.

My friend also made another discovery. Spirit was not only important in general, but the quality of his Spirit was critical to whatever it was he called his job. From this point came a final realization that all those childish things which he put away shortly after reaching the advanced age of 13, were probably the most important foundations for his professional life.

My friend is not alone in his discovery. Some miles away, on the islands of Japan, a new leadership school has been established. Entry into the school, as in all schools in Japan, is a matter of fierce competition, for those who gain admission are expected to constitute a critical piece of the Japanese Leadership: corporate, governmental, and social. One might suspect that the "old view" of leadership is very much operative here, for the selection process is elitist in the extreme, but the program of the school is remarkable. It comes in four parts. Part I is Zen. Part II is everything one might expect to receive in a good business school. Part III involves a year long journey to some other part of the world to see what is going on. And Part IV is a return home to ponder the significance of what has been experienced. It seems that matters of the Spirit are also primary to the Japanese.

In the United States and Western Europe one may gather an infinite number of similar stories. In some cases the stories describe a return to earlier religious traditions, when, like my Indian friend, it is discovered that those childish things of long ago have striking new relevance to the present day. In other cases the tales relate explorations under a number of different banners ranging from the Human Potential Movement to Transpersonal Psychology.

147

I am reminded of a seminar I held for a small number of Dutch executives in the middle 1980's. I was trying my best to gently edge the conversation into a consideration of Transformation and Spirit. After about 20 minutes of going around the barn, one Jean Pierre Guepin, the managing director (CEO) of a global corporation, put up his hand with some impatience. "Stop, Harrison," he said, "We all know Spirit is important, the question is what to do with it." To a surprising extent I think Guepin's premise has been accepted, and we are now seriously about the business of dealing with his question.

The code name for these efforts is *Spirituality*, and it is not uncommon to find references in the serious mainstream journals, and other publications, to spirituality in the workplace, the spiritual aspects of business, and the like. Corporate types pay high prices, and spend long hours, to explore aspects of their being never considered in business school. Not everything, however, that travels under the name of Spirituality is either good or useful. In fact, much is fiction, fraud, or worse. But the interest in Spirit is undeniable.

Many suspect this interest to be essentially escapist, an effort to leave this crazy world in order to find solace and security in a different realm, or an earlier, less tumultuous, time. There are substantial grounds for this suspicion. Indeed, I find the word spirituality of less and less utility, in part because it is "off-putting" to many, but at a deeper level, I think it obscures, even trivializes, the central concern. As we listen to the word in common usage, it most usually appears as an "add-on." We have business, then there is *spiritual business*, relationships, and then *spiritual relationships*. In my experience, Spirit is never an "add-on." It is what is.

THE LEADER'S SPIRIT

So what can we say about the Spirit of Leadership, or the Leader's Spirit? First and most obviously, Spirit is the point of interconnect between us, in our leadership mode, and our fellows. *It is through our Spirit that we participate in the realm of Spirit*. This is our birthright, the commonality of our collective being, the basis from which all of us have, not only the opportunity, but also the responsibility to lead. It comes with our humanity.

There are, of course, a number of ways to insure that the capacity for leadership remains stillborn. At the simplest level, we can deny the presence of Spirit and define our world exclusively in terms of the bits and pieces of our experience, the forms and structures that comprise everyday life. Such a definition locks life into its observable state, with predefined chains of command and levels of authority. In this case only those at the top possess the necessary power and control to make a difference.

We may also abort the appearance of our unique leadership capacity by becoming enmeshed in the age-old discussion about the origin of leadership. Is it *nature or nurture*, born or made? The possibility of discussing this to death is a given, and should we resolve the issue in favor of nature and birth, we may find ourselves excused from the

149

leadership role. I suggest that the distinction is false, and the answer is both. To the extent that we <u>are</u>, and Spirit <u>is</u>, we have everything we need to begin. What happens after that is up to us. The capacity for leadership begins with our humanity, but it only grows with practice and intention.

There are no magic bullets or automatic guarantees when it comes to developing our capacity to lead with Spirit. However, four elements have appeared critical in my experience: (1) Learning About Spirit, (2) Experiencing Spirit, (3) Practice leading with Spirit, and (4) Reprise.

Learning about Spirit

I think it odd that some find the world of Spirit unknown. Awesome for sure, it is hardly strange. For the material on that subject is so voluminous as to boggle the mind. Indeed, I think the case can be made that until fairly recently, even in the West, virtually everything of substance, written or thought, had to do with Spirit, the manifestation of Spirit, or humankind's life as Spirit. If sometimes the subject was approached obliquely or with unfamiliar language, I don't think the authors are to be blamed, and certainly cannot be faulted for lack of effort.

The inherent difficulty of the subject should not surprise us, for in truth it is hard to get mind and words around something that defies comprehension, and transcends verbal description. It might be noted in passing that the contemporary physicists have faced similar problems with comparable results. They have had the audacity to postulate a world that could neither be seen, touched, tasted, or smelled.

And then, with outrageous persistence, they proceeded to describe it. To the uninitiated, the writings of the physicists seem bizarre to the extreme. The mysteries of mathematics aside, the thought that serious people would devote their lives to the study of odd beasties like quarks, neutrinos, and other inhabitants of the subatomic world, is peculiar at best. Few, however, would dismiss the validity of the effort simply on the grounds that it is hard to understand.

The same may be said for Spirit, and for the efforts of those who have made a life study of the subject. In truth we know an enormous amount about Spirit and its operation, but it takes real effort to assimilate that knowledge. In matters of the Spirit, those who refuse to do their homework will have a doubtful grasp of the subject.

Are we then to substitute the Knowledge Elite for the Power Elite? Yes, in the sense that there are guides who may be followed. But no, in the sense that the basis of this knowledge is somehow hidden away from the general population. Unlike the physicists, it is unnecessary to have access to a cyclotron or supercollider in order to join the club. Spirit is everywhere available to anybody who chooses to be open to its presence. Furthermore, the basic manifestations of Spirit are simple in the extreme. We may see it in the lover's touch or the grief of the bereaved. It does not take a graduate degree to perceive its presence. But when one comes to questions such as — What does it mean, where is it going, and (to recall M. Guepin), what do we do with it? — it may be well to consult the work of those who have been there before.

All of which brings up the inevitable question: Where do you start? And the answer is basically, anywhere you like, and more usually, right where you are. You may discover, like my Indian friend, that your discarded tradition is, in fact, a valuable resource. To find out how valuable, you might try a little exercise in which you ask, What is it they (the church fathers, rabbis, gurus etc.) would have thought they were doing, if they had thought what they were doing made sense. It often turns out that what we, in our youth, took to be idiotic obfuscation, actually is quite useful.

In my own case, I don't think it will come as any surprise to reveal that virtually nothing written above is without precedent in the traditions of Christianity, Judaism and their predecessors in the ancient Near East. The whole concept of griefwork assumed early form in the dying and rising God motifs from that area, which were subsequently reformulated in the story of the Crucifixion for Christianity and the Exile for Israel. The story of Spirit has been around for a long time.

If your own tradition seems barren, try the tradition of another, perhaps from the Far East, or the Native Americans, but don't be surprised if you find entry rather rough going. But then, you wouldn't expect to understand quantum mechanics on your first day in class.

If you stay the course, and don't give up the first time you run into an unpronounceable word, be prepared for an interesting surprise. As different as the several traditions may be, their similarities are often more striking. This fact was driven home in conversation with some of my Buddhist and Hindu colleagues, who at various times have accused me of reading deeply in their sacred traditions. Nothing could be further from the truth, for although I have read and benefited much, my real exposure is only a mile wide and an inch deep.

152

The equation occurs not on the level of the traditions in question, but rather in terms of what we all share in common: Spirit. So start anywhere you want, with a reasonable expectation of arrival at all other points. [20]

Experience Spirit

No book in the world can substitute for the experience of Spirit, and your opportunities to have that experience are limited only by your willingness to try.

Take any moment in time, this one, for example. Close your eyes, breath deeply, and imagine the face of one you love. Let the memories pass through, of all the places you went, and the things you did. Don't hold on to any of those, just let them go. Concentrate on the face, and let it be there. If you are not careful, you will encounter their Spirit. Stripped of time and space, elevated above the comings and goings of daily life, Spirit is. And beneath the Spirit of that person is a larger world of Spirit, which you may sense but not know. Try it. Spirit is available whenever we are available to it. It is not so much a matter of taking a lot of time, but having intention.

A silly mind game perhaps, but it is often necessary to trick the mind into stopping thinking, for thoughts, more often than not, get in the way of Spirit. Invoking Spirit, however, is not a party game, and although the little exercise I have suggested above may bring you to the edge of Spirit, it cannot

[20] I have included in the bibliography a number of books that have been helpful to me. That is no guarantee that they will suit you. If you are looking for a place to start your own exploration of Spirit, however, these authors may be useful.

substitute for more extended practice, which is what meditation (by whatever name or form) is all about.

At this point, I can imagine some of you smiling knowingly as if to say, I knew it, sooner or later he was going to have us in the Lotus Position. Frankly, I can't get into the Lotus Position, and although it has proven useful for many generations of experienced Spirit watchers, it is not my cup of tea, nor do I believe it essential for the process. But disciplined practice is. Since there are any number of classes and teachers, usually no further away than your local church, synagogue or temple, suggesting one, or several, is hardly to the point. But if one does not work, do not despair, just keep your eyes open. Following the footprints of Spirit requires practice, and as any athlete knows, disciplined exercise is essential, but not all exercise forms are appropriate for you. Keep looking.

Given the fact that we have a world seemingly bent on collective suicide, to say nothing of a business environment apparently out to destroy us, you may wonder how you can afford the apparent luxury of Spirit-watching. I can only suggest that under the circumstances you can't afford NOT to. The next time you find yourself in the caldron of change, which is likely to be tomorrow morning, with responsibility for yourself and colleagues, being able to intuit the flow of Spirit in others, and to ground, or center, Spirit in yourself, is likely to make the difference between realizing new opportunity and chalking up disaster. I don't think you can afford to be ill-prepared.

Practice Leading

There is a general myth of powerlessness, and even such enlightened folks as the readers of this book, are likely to fall prey. It is, after all, easier, more advisable, or appropriate, to leave leadership to others. Others can then assume the blame. We all do it, but I think you will agree that the time for such self-indulgence is rapidly running out.

Even when we have cast off the myth of powerlessness, the temptation is always to wait for the "Big One," that moment in history when the trumpets sound, and we are called to the battlements. Unfortunately, when that moment arrives, we are usually not ready. We must take the opportunity to practice leadership whenever, and wherever, we are.

For example, the next time a friend or colleague is "terminated," you will have the chance to Be with them through Shock, Anger, Memories, down into the dumps, on to Open Space, Imagination and Vision. Take the opportunity to practice creating space, and always ask questions. Check the flow of Spirit and see what happens should you start providing answers and not questions. Check your own Spirit for those telltale signs of anxiety which seemingly force you to exercise CONTROL.

Or let's say you are part of a secretarial pool, or a small design team. For a while now you have been doing the same thing, and doing it very well, so well in fact that you actually enjoy what you are doing. Then one day, from the Olympian heights, comes the word. The group is through, the work is done. It's all over, baby. Guess what? You have another opportunity to help your fellows and yourself, while simultaneously enhancing your capacity for leadership. The occasion for practice is omnipresent, regardless of your perceived station in life. Whether you are on top of the heap, or scarcely on the playing field, the opportunities are there.

And what does all this have to do with imminent global disaster? Nothing and everything. Quite obviously your friend's job loss or the demise of your working group will probably have minuscule impact on the global scene. But every time we practice and develop our innate capacity for leadership, it can only improve, so that when the Big One does come, as it probably will, we will be ready. And when might that be? Who knows, even as the two young ladies at OCF could have had no premonition that they were going to exercise such a major role in the turnaround of Spirit in that place.

Even if the Big One never comes, practice is not in vain. For I think you will discover that as you enrich the Spirit of others, so your own Spirit will grow. And who knows, perhaps it is not your role to lead the charge, but rather to feed the ball to those who will. Whoever has the ball is leader, but as we know by now, ball hogs die.

Reprise

As Rome was not built in a day, so our capacity for leadership is not brought to peak performance with a single iteration from learning, to experience, and on to practice. It is only when our practice of leadership is repetitively grounded in our learning, as enriched by our experience, that peak levels begin to emerge. There are no magic wands here, nor is there any cause for despair. The leadership we need is available in all of us. We have only to make it manifest.

The leadership
we need is available in all of us.

WE HAVE ONLY TO MAKE IT
MANIFEST.

Selected Bibliography

Bateson, Gregory, <u>Mind and Nature</u>, Bantam/New Age, 1980.

_____, <u>Steps Towards and Ecology of Mind</u>,
Ballentine Books, 1972.

Ferguson, Marilyn, <u>The Aquarian Conspiracy</u>. Tarcher, 1980.

Goldberg, Philip, <u>The Intuitive Edge</u>, Tarcher, 1983.

Harman, Willis and Rheingold, Howard, <u>Higher Creativity</u>,
Tarcher, 1984.

Kübler-Ross, Elizabeth, <u>On Death and Dying</u>, Macmillan paper
back, 1970.

Kuhn, Thomas, <u>The Structure of Scientific Revolutions</u>,
University of Chicago, 1970.

Prigogine, Ilya, <u>Order out of Chaos</u>, Bantam New Age, 1984.

Tillich, Paul, <u>The Courage to Be</u>, Yale University Press, 1952

Whitmont, Edward, <u>Return of the Goddess</u>, Crossroad, 1982.

Wilber, Ken, <u>No Boundary,</u> Shambala, 1981.

_____, <u>The Spectrum of Consciousness</u>, Quest, 1977.

_____, <u>Up From Eden</u>, Anchor Press/Doubleday, 1981.